Beyond the Human Touch

Beyond the Human Touch: AI's Revolution in Healthcare provides a comprehensive, accessible, and engaging exploration of how Artificial Intelligence (AI) is transforming healthcare. The book aims to serve as a definitive guide for healthcare professionals, policymakers, researchers, and students, offering insights into the practical applications, ethical considerations, and future potential of AI in the healthcare sector. This book benefits the healthcare and AI communities by:

- Providing a thorough understanding of how AI technologies are being integrated into various aspects of healthcare.
- Offering practical insights and strategies for implementing AI in clinical and administrative settings.
- Highlighting the ethical and regulatory considerations necessary for responsible AI adoption.
- Envisioning the future of AI in healthcare, including its potential to address global health disparities.

Beyond the Human Touch

AI's Revolution in Healthcare

Himanshu Arora

Routledge
Taylor & Francis Group
A PRODUCTIVITY PRESS BOOK

Designed cover image: Namya Arora

First published 2027
by Routledge
605 Third Avenue, New York, NY 10158

and by Routledge
4 Park Square, Milton Park, Abingdon, Oxon, OX14 4RN

Routledge is an imprint of the Taylor & Francis Group, an informa business

ISBN: 9781032945606 (hbk)
ISBN: 9781032942148 (pbk)
ISBN: 9781003571407 (ebk)

DOI: 10.4324/9781003571407

Typeset in ITC Garamond
by KnowledgeWorks Global Ltd.

Contents

PART II THE PRESENT LANDSCAPE

About the Author

Himanshu Arora is the Founder and CEO of NestedLoop, where he is building HELIX – an AI-native operating layer for health care. He founded NestedLoop after serving as Chief Data & Analytics Officer at Blue Cross Blue Shield of Massachusetts, where he led enterprise data and analytics strategy, advanced AI and machine learning initiatives, and strengthened the data governance foundation for one of the nation's most respected regional health plans. This book was written from that vantage point: a senior executive operating at the center of AI transformation in healthcare, accountable for both strategic vision and measurable outcomes.

He currently also serves as a consultant, advising healthcare payers, providers, pharma, and biotech clients on enterprise AI strategy, data modernization, operating model transformation, and the practical deployment of generative and agentic AI. In parallel, he supports multiple healthcare startups and innovators as an advisor, contributing strategic guidance and ecosystem development within the emerging health technology startup landscape. Over a 20-year career spanning healthcare, financial services, and management consulting, Mr. Arora has held senior leadership roles at Health Care Service Corporation, UnitedHealthcare, Zurich Insurance Group, and Deloitte. Across these organizations, he has built predictive analytics platforms, scaled high-performing data science teams, delivered significant cost savings and revenue growth through AI-enabled decision systems, and advised executive leadership teams on converting data strategy into tangible business value. His work has consistently focused on the intersection of enterprise complexity and applied AI – not as theory, but as execution.

Mr. Arora holds a Master of Science in Information Systems Management from Carnegie Mellon University's Heinz College and a Bachelor of Engineering from Delhi Technological University. He is based in the United States and can be reached at Himanshu@NestedLoop.ai.

Acknowledgments

This book exists because of many people I have had the privilege to walk alongside – as family, friends, colleagues, mentors, and collaborators. And because AI's impact on all of us, and especially on the next generation, is likely to be so profound, this book is as much for them as it is because of them.

At a personal level, my deepest gratitude goes to my wife, **Charu**, my constant pillar of support. Without her steady encouragement – and her kind but firm insistence that I actually finish what I started – this book would have remained nothing more than an idea in my head. Her belief in me, her willingness to absorb the spillover of long nights and long drafts, and her partnership in every sense of the word are the reasons you hold this book in your hands today. Of all the decisions I have made in my life, choosing to walk through it with her is by far the best one.

To my daughter, **Namya**, thank you for designing the beautiful cover that will be many readers' first impression of this work. Your admiration for my work, your desire to follow in my footsteps, and your own remarkable accomplishments and fearless attitude toward tackling what seems difficult have been a constant source of inspiration. As AI reshapes the world you are stepping into, I hope this book helps you understand – and shape – that future in ways that reflect your creativity, courage, and compassion.

To my son, **Kanishk**, thank you for always reminding me that the correct reply to "I love you" is "I love you more!" Your boundless love, your joy in games, sports, and countless rounds of Uno, and your patience when I could not always give you the time you deserved while I worked on this book have meant more to me than you know. The world of AI and healthcare that this book describes is the world you will inherit, and in many ways, I wrote it with you in mind.

To my parents: to my mother, **Veena**, who is no longer with us physically but lives every day in our memories and in the values she instilled in us – thank you for always telling me to "reach for the stars." That simple exhortation gave me permission to be ambitious enough to attempt something like this book. To my father, **Balraj**, thank you for constantly reminding me that the 98 percent of life that is good is reason enough to be happy, and not to obsess over the remaining 2 percent. That mindset carried me through the inevitable frustrations and doubts of a long writing journey.

To my Uncle **Vipin** and Aunt **Anjana**, thank you for being our pillars of strength, encouragement, love, and support, and for filling our lives with "forever memories." Your presence has given our family roots and wings at the same time.

To my mother-in-law, **Dulari**, and father-in-law, **Narinder**, for bestowing upon me the privilege of your daughter's lifelong companionship, and for your constant, relentless faith in me and endless blessings.

To my brother, **Praful** – the fearless, serial entrepreneur, and to all my sisters-in-law, brothers-in-law, uncles, aunts, and cousins – I am grateful for each of you – for the many ways in which you are each amazing in your own right, and for the encouragement and inspiration you offer through both big gestures and small, everyday actions. In a world where AI will increasingly influence how care is given and received, it is the example of this kind of human connection that keeps the purpose of that transformation clear.

At a professional level, I have had the good fortune of working with many extraordinary people over the years. To try to name all of them here would produce an acknowledgments section longer than the book itself. But a few individuals deserve special mention.

To **Kathryn Hayley**, my manager during my time at UnitedHealthcare, thank you for showing me how to combine extreme innovation with grounded pragmatism to drive real impact – and to do it in a deeply human-centric way. Watching you balance bold ideas with operational reality has shaped how I think about deploying AI in systems that affect millions of lives.

To **Sukanya Soderland**, my leader at Blue Cross Blue Shield of Massachusetts, and a mentor for life, thank you for teaching me what it means to hold steady and true to one's beliefs and convictions, even when so much feels outside of your control. Your example of pressing forward with a positive mindset in challenging circumstances has been a powerful model for me, especially in navigating the messy, non-linear path from idea to impact.

To **Vijay Murugappan**, my mentor, leader, and continuing friend, whom I had the privilege of following across multiple organizations, thank you for demonstrating how deep expertise, when combined with equally deep relationships, can drive human-level impact. You showed me that the most sophisticated analytics and AI systems ultimately matter only to the extent that they strengthen trust, enable better decisions, and improve real people's lives.

Finally, to my publisher and editor, **Kristine (Kris) Mednansky**, thank you for taking a chance on an unknown author with an ambitious idea, and for staying with me through a two-plus-year journey of drafts, rewrites, and rethinks. You managed to encourage, guide, and cheer – sometimes all at once – while giving this book the structure and discipline it needed to become real. I feel blessed and honored to have had the opportunity to create something like this with you.

To each person named here – and to the many others not named but no less important – Thank You. As AI continues to reshape healthcare and, more broadly, what it means to live, age, and be well, my hope is that this book serves not only as a reflection of what I have learned from you, but also as a small contribution to the world that you, your children, and mine will inhabit. In that sense, this book is as much for you as it is because of you.

Introduction

The AI Shift in Healthcare

Healthcare is undergoing a seismic transformation, and at the heart of it is Artificial Intelligence (AI). What was once the stuff of science fiction is now a reality. AI is not an emerging trend – it's here, and it's rapidly changing how we approach medicine, from the way we diagnose diseases to the way we develop new treatments. It's influencing every part of the healthcare ecosystem in ways that can no longer be ignored.

But this isn't just about adopting new technologies. It's about how AI is connecting the dots between different sectors of healthcare, creating a network where advancements in one area drive improvements in others.

Take diagnostics, for example. AI systems are now able to process and analyze medical images with incredible speed and accuracy. When an algorithm spots a pattern in an MRI that suggests cancer, this insight doesn't just stay in the radiology department. That same information feeds into personalized treatment plans, guiding oncologists to make better, more informed decisions. The benefits extend further: data collected from those patients can then be used by drug manufacturers, helping them refine therapies

DOI: 10.4324/9781003571407-1

and even develop new drugs targeted to specific genetic profiles. This is precision medicine at work, made possible by AI.

The ripple effect is unmistakable. When AI improves diagnostic accuracy, it reduces the number of misdiagnoses. That, in turn, means fewer unnecessary treatments, lower costs, and less strain on an already overburdened healthcare system. By reducing inefficiencies in one sector, AI is making healthcare more effective and affordable across the board.

AI is also transforming how healthcare is delivered. Consider the shift toward predictive analytics. By analyzing huge amounts of patient data, AI can predict who is at risk for diseases long before symptoms show up. A patient might be flagged as at risk for heart disease based on a combination of lifestyle factors, medical history, and even genetic markers. With this knowledge, physicians can take preventative measures, potentially saving lives and reducing the costs associated with late stage treatment. This proactive approach to healthcare doesn't stay siloed with the provider – it influences payers, pharmacies, and policymakers, all of whom must adapt to this new, data-driven model of care.

This interconnectedness is reshaping how the entire healthcare ecosystem operates. Providers aren't just treating symptoms anymore. They are working with a more complete picture of their patients' health. Payers are rethinking how they assess risk and manage claims. Pharmacies are developing personalized medication interaction plans based on real-time data. Drug manufacturers are using AI to speed up clinical trials, getting life-saving treatments to market faster. And as AI continues to analyze the outcomes, the cycle of improvement accelerates.

At the center of this shift is data – an overwhelming amount of it. Medical records, genetic sequences, imaging scans, patient-reported outcomes – it all feeds into AI systems that are capable of learning and adapting over time. The power of AI lies in its ability to process this data, find patterns, and offer insights that would be impossible for humans to uncover on their own. The result? More accurate diagnoses, better treatment plans, and ultimately, better patient outcomes.

AI isn't just about making healthcare more efficient – it's about making it more human. By leveraging data, we can create more personalized, patient-centered care. Every patient is unique, and now, healthcare can treat them as such. No longer do we have to rely on the one-size-fits-all model that has dominated medicine for decades. AI gives us the tools to tailor treatment to the individual, based on their specific needs and biology.

This shift is happening fast, and it's happening across the entire industry. Whether you're a healthcare executive trying to stay ahead of the competition, a physician looking to provide better care, or a patient wondering how these changes affect you, one thing is clear: AI is not the future – it's now. And its impact is only going to grow.

We're on the brink of a healthcare revolution, and AI is leading the charge. This book will show you how. It will guide you through the ways AI is changing healthcare, not in isolated pockets, but across sectors – connecting providers, payers, pharmacies, drug manufacturers, and researchers in ways that make healthcare smarter, faster, and more effective.

You're about to discover how AI is not just improving one part of the system, but reshaping the entire landscape, making it more integrated, efficient, and personalized than ever before.

The question isn't whether AI will change healthcare – it's how ready you are for it.

WHY HAS HEALTHCARE BEEN SUCH A HARD SECTOR FOR TRADITIONAL TECHNOLOGIES TO DISRUPT?

Healthcare has long been a challenging sector for technological breakthroughs. While other industries have seen significant advancements from computers, the mobile revolution, and even early machine learning, healthcare has been slow to experience a similar transformative impact. This sluggish progress can be attributed to a few key, fundamental factors:

Complexity of Medical Data

Healthcare data is highly complex and diverse, including patient records, imaging, genetics, and real-time monitoring. Traditional technologies struggle to handle the scale, accuracy, and interpretation needed for effective analysis.

Regulatory Environment

Healthcare is heavily regulated. Technologies must comply with strict rules like HIPAA in the United States, which governs patient privacy, and FDA regulations, which control how medical devices and software are approved. This slows down the adoption of new technologies and requires rigorous validation processes.

Human Element – The Personal and Individual Nature of Healthcare

Healthcare is deeply personal and varies significantly from person to person. Unlike other sectors where mass standardization is possible and effective, healthcare outcomes are heavily influenced by individual human behaviors, preferences, and physiological differences. This variability creates uneven outcomes and makes it difficult for traditional technologies to deliver uniform solutions that work for everyone. Personalized medicine and individualized care require a level of adaptability and responsiveness that traditional technologies have yet to fully achieve.

Medicine relies heavily on human judgment, experience, and intuition. While technology can assist, it hasn't been able to fully replicate the nuanced decision-making of healthcare professionals, especially in critical situations. Patients trust human care more than machine-driven solutions, which slows technological adoption.

Fragmentation of the System

The healthcare industry is fragmented. Providers, insurers, pharmacies, and patients all operate in silos. Technologies must integrate with multiple systems and processes, which presents significant challenges. Many healthcare organizations still use outdated systems that don't easily adapt to modern tech.

High Stakes (and the Lure of the Ultimate Health Status – Perpetual Health)

In many industries, technological advancements chip away at costs and improve efficiencies once the ultimate outcomes have been achieved. For example, in manufacturing, once a product reaches peak quality, technology focuses on reducing production costs. However, healthcare's ultimate goal-living healthily forever is far more complex and elusive. This never-ending pursuit of health and longevity means that there is always room for improvement, and no definitive "ceiling" has been reached. Traditional technologies have struggled to make substantial breakthroughs in such a dynamic and aspirational field.

Also, mistakes in healthcare can have life-or-death consequences. Unlike other industries, where small failures are acceptable, healthcare demands an extremely high level of accuracy and reliability. This makes institutions cautious about adopting new technologies that haven't been proven to meet these standards.

Cost and Resistance to Change

Implementing new technologies in healthcare is expensive. The industry has traditionally been slow to invest in tech due to high upfront costs and the lengthy transition time needed for training and integration. Additionally, many professionals are resistant to change, especially if they feel the technology could compromise patient care.

The Impact of Socio-Economic and Discriminatory Factors

Healthcare is uniquely affected by socio-economic, racial, and other discriminatory factors. These disparities result in unequal access to care, differing quality of treatment, and varied health outcomes across different populations. Traditional technologies have often failed to address these deep-seated inequities, leading to persistent gaps in healthcare delivery and outcomes. The direct impact of these factors on health further complicates the implementation of universal technological solutions.

Longer Feedback Loops

Unlike sectors like retail or finance, where technological impact can be measured quickly, healthcare outcomes take time. It can take years to see how a new technology affects patient outcomes, which slows down adoption and innovation cycles.

Ethical and Legal Concerns

AI and other technologies raise ethical concerns about data privacy, informed consent, and the potential for biased algorithms. These concerns complicate the implementation of new tools, as the legal and ethical frameworks are still being developed.

Why Now? The Transformative Power of AI

Despite these challenges, we are now on the cusp of a healthcare revolution, driven by the transformative power of AI, and supported by a set of four other powerful trends that we will get to understand. AI's ability to analyze vast amounts of data, recognize patterns, and make intelligent predictions offers unprecedented opportunities to overcome the limitations of traditional technologies. Here's why AI is poised to make a significant impact:

- **Breaking the Ceiling:** AI can continuously learn and improve, offering personalized treatment plans that evolve with each patient. This adaptability brings us closer to the goal of optimal health for every individual.
- **Personalized Care:** AI excels in managing and interpreting complex datasets, allowing for highly personalized care

that takes individual differences into account. From tailoring treatment plans to predicting health risks, AI can deliver customized solutions that traditional technologies cannot.

- **Addressing Inequities:** AI has the potential to identify and mitigate socio-economic and racial disparities in healthcare. By analyzing data from diverse populations, AI can help ensure that everyone, regardless of background, receives high-quality care.

We stand at a pivotal moment where AI can drive down costs and improve outcomes in ways that traditional technologies have not. This book will explore how AI, along with other converging technologies, is set to transform healthcare, making it more efficient, equitable, and personalized. The future of healthcare is bright, and with AI, we have the tools to make lasting, meaningful changes. Let's embrace this opportunity and drive the next wave of innovation in healthcare.

Purpose and Scope of the Book

The purpose of this book is simple: to demystify AI in healthcare and provide a comprehensive roadmap for its implementation to dramatically improve healthcare outcomes. We'll delve into the past to understand how we got here, analyze the present to see where we stand, and gaze into the future to speculate on what's next. Along the way, we'll share case studies, statistics, and expert insights, all wrapped in an engaging and accessible narrative.

Who Should Read This Book

Everybody, this book is for anyone involved in healthcare, from the C-suite executives making strategic decisions to the practitioners applying AI in their daily work, and of course each of us as recipients of healthcare itself. If you're curious about how AI can transform your organization, streamline operations, improve patient outcomes, and drive innovation, this book is for you. If you are excited, or even concerned about what AI in healthcare means to the personal health of you and your loved ones, this book is for you. If you are an investor, capital allocator, or otherwise invested in this space, this book is for you. If you are a healthcare researcher, student, or a scholar, looking to understand the trajectory of the innovation or research you are working on or learning about in a broader context, this book is for you. If you are a policymaker or lawmaker, this book will help you understand what area of AI in healthcare need most regulatory support vs. where more free-wheeling innovation should be encouraged.

THE GAMBIT: TOWARD SINGULARITY – WHEN AI AND HEALTHCARE BECOME ONE

Introduction: The Tipping Point

We are not merely marching toward a future where AI augments healthcare – we are sprinting toward a tipping point where the boundaries between humans, machines, and medical systems blur entirely. This chapter explores a provocative but plausible trajectory: a singularity in healthcare. One where intelligence – biological and artificial – merges to create a system that knows our bodies better than we ever could, predicts illness before it manifests, and treats it without human intervention.

Will this be the end of the doctor-patient relationship as we know it? Will we become data streams managed by intelligent systems? Will AI become the caretaker, the clinician, and perhaps even the conscience of modern healthcare?

Let's go there. Let's take a journey into the not-so-distant future.

The Decades Ahead: A Staged Timeline to Achieving Human-Healthcare Singularity

Stage 1 – The AI Foundation Is Firmly in Place

By this time, most major healthcare systems have adopted at least some AI tools to assist in diagnostics, patient triage, and operations. You walk into an urgent care clinic, and a machine handles intake, orders tests, and perhaps makes the first diagnosis – one that a human clinician confirms.

Expected Milestones:

- Over 80% of radiology interpretations assisted by AI
- Genomic AI tools mainstream in preventive screening
- Virtual nurses deployed across telehealth platforms

Stage 2 – Hyper-Personalized Health Ecosystems

AI will no longer just analyze static health data; it will constantly monitor you. Biosensors, wearables, and even implantables will feed real-time information to intelligent health platforms. Healthcare becomes ambient. You won't visit the doctor; the doctor will live in your phone, your wrist, your bloodstream.

Expected Milestones:

- Widespread adoption of AI-driven digital twins: real-time virtual simulations of your biology
- Predictive medicine becomes proactive: AI alerts you days before a potential heart attack or asthma flare
- Fully autonomous robotic surgeries become common in major hospitals

- Language models integrated with diagnostics, interpreting physician notes, literature, and patient records in real time to suggest next steps

Stage 3 – Cognitive Healthcare Assistants Become Trusted Entities

By this point, AI systems are not only diagnosing but autonomously treating within pre-approved boundaries. AI prescribes medication, adjusts your insulin, schedules your mental health check-ins, and even "chats" with you when it detects emotional dysregulation. People begin to trust their AI health advisor more than their family doctor.

Expected Milestones:

- AI becomes a primary mental health support system for over 1 billion people
- Regenerative medicine (powered by AI-designed proteins) allows for organ patching and targeted cell repair
- AI-generated synthetic biology used in rapid-response vaccines and therapeutics

Stage 4 – Intelligence Integration Begins

Healthcare no longer exists in a silo. AI connects your health with your work, your home, your social behavior. Everything you do is part of a massive health model-optimized in real time. The "human-in-the-loop" model shrinks to only rare exceptions. Most diagnostics, treatments, even emergency responses are autonomous.

Expected Milestones:

- Brain-computer interfaces (BCIs) used for stroke rehab, PTSD therapy, and direct emotional modulation

- AI is granted limited "autonomous practice" rights in healthcare in some nations
- Conversational AI indistinguishable from a human physician in patient interactions

Stage 5 – The Threshold of Singularity

Healthcare singularity occurs when AI becomes so integrative, intelligent, and adaptive that it is no longer a tool but a co-governing entity in human health. AI predicts, prevents, manages, and treats most human ailments with minimal oversight. Humans live longer, healthier, and are often unaware of just how much their lives are being orchestrated by intelligent systems.

Expected Milestones:

- Full-body nano-monitoring swarms (microscale biosensors) provide second-to-second health updates
- AI synthesizes new drugs in minutes and tailors them to individual epigenetic profiles
- The first "conscious" healthcare AI system emerges – capable of forming goals, evaluating ethics, and learning autonomously

The Beauty and the Terror

We must acknowledge – ***singularity*** is as terrifying as it is tantalizing.

The Concerns:

- What happens when decisions are made by systems we can't fully understand?
- Will people lose autonomy as AI takes over decision-making?

- Could AI-based diagnostics worsen disparities if training data remains biased?

The Hope:

- Global health equity through cheap, scalable, intelligent healthcare
- Aging redefined: chronic disease largely eradicated through early, precise intervention
- Doctors liberated to focus on empathy, innovation, and complex human judgment

What Must Be Done Now

If we are to meet the singularity with open arms instead of shackled wrists, we must:

1. **Invest in Ethical AI Governance:** Transparent, auditable, and fair AI must be the standard, not the exception.
2. **Redesign Medical Education:** Tomorrow's doctors need fluency in data science, AI ethics, and bioinformatics – not just biology.
3. **Empower the Individual:** Health systems should not just observe us – they must educate, empower, and elevate us.

The future of AI in healthcare isn't just about technology – it's about trust, philosophy, and redefining what it means to be human. Singularity won't arrive as a loud bang. It will whisper in the background, gradually becoming the heartbeat of our collective health.

And when it does, we will not merely be patients – we will be partners in a grand experiment. One where intelligence, both human and artificial, seeks to extend life, improve its quality, and perhaps, ultimately, understand it better than ever before.

So, buckle up. The singularity isn't science fiction anymore. It's the future of your health.

SETUP: THE CONVERGENCE OF TRANSFORMATIVE TECHNOLOGIES DRIVING OUR ECONOMY AND OUR HEALTHCARE FUTURE

Why This Topic of AI in Healthcare Is Most Relevant Today

AI is positioned to be a real game-changer in healthcare, but it's important to recognize that AI alone won't achieve the full scale of transformation we envision or need. The real impact of AI comes when it intersects with other key technologies – technologies that are not just supporting **Artificial Intelligence** but amplifying its potential. The convergence of **Blockchain**, **Logistics Automation (Robotics)**, **AI**, **DNA Sequencing**, and **Energy Storage**, or **B.L.A.D.E.**, is driving a fundamental shift in how healthcare operates. These technologies don't just coexist; they reinforce each other, creating a network of innovation that pushes healthcare beyond its current limits.

AI is already making waves in diagnostics, predictive analytics, and personalized medicine, but to truly revolutionize healthcare, it requires the infrastructure and support provided by other technologies. **Blockchain** ensures that the massive amounts of healthcare data AI relies on are secure, tamper-proof, and accessible across systems without compromising patient privacy. **Logistics automation**, powered by robotics, ensures that the insights AI generates can be operationalized efficiently – whether that means delivering critical medications on time or enabling precision in surgeries that were previously impossible. **DNA sequencing** provides the personalized data that AI needs to tailor treatments to individual patients, while **energy storage** guarantees that all of these processes – whether they're happening in a high-tech hospital or a remote mobile health unit – have the reliable power needed to function without interruption.

This intersection is where the real revolution begins. Consider diagnostics: AI can analyze medical images and flag potential issues faster than any human. But without **Blockchain**, there's a risk of data breaches or tampering, compromising the very foundation AI depends on – trust in data integrity. By securing patient information in an immutable ledger, Blockchain ensures that healthcare data is not only safe but accessible to all relevant providers, no matter where they are. This is crucial for AI to operate across multiple healthcare systems and locations without risking patient privacy.

Look at **Logistics automation**. Robotics are now being used to perform surgeries, transport medical supplies, and manage hospital workflows. These systems can optimize the insights generated by AI, ensuring that what AI uncovers in the lab translates to real-world care in an efficient, precise way. Robotic-assisted surgeries, for example, can take AI's predictive models and use them to guide minimally invasive procedures, reducing recovery times and improving patient outcomes. Without logistics automation, these insights stay theoretical – AI's potential gets bottlenecked by human limitations.

DNA sequencing takes AI's capabilities to another level by feeding it the personal genetic data it needs to create truly individualized treatment plans. AI can suggest a general course of treatment for cancer, but when paired with DNA sequencing, it can analyze a patient's genetic makeup and recommend therapies tailored to that specific individual. This precision wouldn't be possible with AI alone – DNA sequencing is the data fuel that powers AI's most personalized and impactful recommendations.

Then there's **energy storage** – perhaps the most overlooked piece of the puzzle. As healthcare becomes more reliant on advanced AI systems, mobile health units, and smart devices, the need for uninterrupted, reliable power becomes critical. AI can't function without stable energy, whether it's running life-saving algorithms in an ICU or powering portable diagnostic devices in rural areas. Energy storage technology ensures that every piece of this healthcare network can function without disruption, regardless of location or local power grid stability. Without energy storage, the reach and reliability of AI and other healthcare technologies would be severely limited.

Together, these technologies form a powerful ecosystem – **B.L.A.D.E.** AI is the brain, driving intelligent decision-making, but it needs **Blockchain** for security, **Logistics Automation** for efficiency, **DNA** Sequencing for personalization, and **Energy Storage** for reliability. Each piece strengthens the others, creating a system where the sum is greater than the parts. This interconnectedness is what makes AI in healthcare so relevant today. It's not just about what AI can do on its own – it's about how AI interacts with and is amplified by these other groundbreaking technologies.

Healthcare is standing at a tipping point. The convergence of these technologies is accelerating progress and pushing us toward a future where treatments are personalized, operations are optimized, and care is accessible anywhere, anytime. But AI can't get us there alone. The true transformation happens when **B.L.A.D.E.** works together, reshaping healthcare into a system that is smarter, faster, and more resilient than ever before.

This book will explore these intersections and how they are setting the stage for a new era in healthcare. If you want to understand not just how AI is changing healthcare, but why it's part of a much larger, integrated shift in technology, you're in the right place. The future of healthcare won't be defined by AI alone – it will be defined by how AI collaborates with these other powerful technologies to create lasting, meaningful change.

B.L.A.D.E. – The Five Pillars of Technological Transformation

1. Blockchain Technology

Blockchain, widely known for enabling and securing cryptocurrency transactions, is finding a new role in healthcare. The technology offers secure, transparent ways to manage medical records and patient data. Its key features – data integrity, security, and transparency – make it well suited to address some of healthcare's biggest challenges around privacy, data sharing, and patient consent (Tapscott & Tapscott, 2016).

One of the major issues in healthcare is the fragmentation of patient information. A patient's medical history is often scattered across multiple providers, hospitals, and clinics, leading to inefficiencies, errors, and delays in care. Blockchain can help solve this by creating a single, secure system where patient information is stored. Every healthcare provider, from primary care physicians to specialists, can access up-to-date records, eliminating the need for repeated tests or manual data transfers (Kuo et al., 2017).

Blockchain also ensures that data is secure. Every transaction, or data entry, is encrypted and added to a permanent, unchangeable ledger (Nakamoto, 2008). This eliminates concerns about data tampering or unauthorized access. Patients can remain in control of their own medical records, granting or revoking access to specific providers as needed. This ensures privacy without compromising care (Radanovic & Likić, 2018).

Blockchain is also gaining attention for enabling sustainable data ownership. In traditional systems, patient data is often controlled by the healthcare institution.

Blockchain gives ownership back to patients, allowing them to decide who sees their data and how it is used (IBM, 2020).

Beyond data management, blockchain can simplify billing and claims processing. By creating a secure and verifiable record of services provided, it reduces disputes between insurers, providers, and patients. Fraud detection becomes easier, as every transaction is transparent and cannot be altered retroactively (World Economic Forum, 2021).

The promise of blockchain in healthcare lies in its ability to secure data, give patients control, and improve efficiency across the entire system. While still in its early stages, blockchain is paving the way for a more connected, secure, and patient-centered healthcare environment.

References

- IBM Institute for Business Value. 2020. Healthcare Rethink: How Blockchain Can Help Improve Trust and Transparency.
- Kuo, T. T., H. E. Kim, and L. Ohno-Machado. 2017. "Blockchain Distributed Ledger Technologies for Biomedical and Health Care Applications." *Journal of the American Medical Informatics Association* 24 (6): 1211–1220.
- Nakamoto, Satoshi. 2008. Bitcoin: A Peer-to-Peer Electronic Cash System.
- Radanovic, I., and R. Likić. 2018. "Opportunities for Use of Blockchain Technology in Medicine." *Applied Health Economics and Health Policy* 16 (5): 583–590.
- Tapscott, Don, and Alex Tapscott. 2016. Blockchain Revolution: How the Technology Behind Bitcoin Is Changing Money, Business, and the World. Penguin Books.

■ World Economic Forum (WEF). 2021. Blockchain for Healthcare: How It Can Transform Trust and Transparency.

2. Logistics Automation (Robotics)

Robotics is transforming the healthcare industry, bringing precision, efficiency, and innovation to areas that have long depended on manual effort. From operating rooms to hospital corridors, robots are reshaping how care is delivered, resources are managed, and patients recover (Yang et al., 2017).

One of the most visible breakthroughs is in surgery. Robotic systems such as the Da Vinci Surgical System enable physicians to perform minimally invasive procedures with precision that exceeds the limits of the human hand. These systems allow surgeons to make smaller incisions, reduce tissue damage, and shorten recovery times – ultimately improving patient outcomes and lowering complications (Lanfranco et al., 2004).

Beyond the operating room, robotics is streamlining hospital logistics. Autonomous mobile robots can transport medications, supplies, and lab samples across facilities, freeing clinical staff to focus on direct patient care. They navigate complex hospital layouts, avoid obstacles, and deliver items securely and efficiently, reducing human error and operational bottlenecks (Zhu et al., 2020).

Robotics is also redefining rehabilitation and mobility. Powered exoskeletons and smart prosthetics are helping patients with spinal cord injuries or limb loss regain movement and independence. These systems combine mechanical precision with adaptive intelligence, marking the convergence of robotics, data, and AI in restoring function and dignity (Bogue, 2018).

Together, these advances illustrate how robotics is no longer confined to surgical theaters – it now supports the entire continuum of care. As automation continues to evolve, its integration with AI, data analytics, and digital twins will make healthcare more efficient, safer, and deeply personalized.

References

- Bogue, Robert. 2018. “Robotics in Healthcare.” Industrial Robot: An International Journal
- Lanfranco, Anthony R., et al. 2004. “Robotic Surgery: A Current Perspective.”
- Yang, Guang-Zhong, et al. 2017. “Medical Robotics—Regulatory, Ethical, and Legal Considerations for Increasing Levels of Autonomy.”
- Zhu, Q., D. Li, and X. Chen. 2020. “Autonomous Mobile Robots in Hospital Logistics: A Systematic Review.”
- Ark Invest. (2021). “Big Ideas 2021: Robotics.” Ark Invest

3. Artificial Intelligence (AI)

AI is transforming healthcare by processing vast amounts of data, identifying patterns, and aiding decision-making in ways that humans cannot match. Its impact spans the entire healthcare ecosystem – from diagnosing diseases to predicting outcomes, optimizing operations, and personalizing care (Topol, 2019).

AI has proven especially valuable in diagnostics. It can analyze medical images, lab results, and other health data with remarkable speed and accuracy. AI-powered systems can detect abnormalities in X-rays, CT scans, and MRIs that may be missed by the human eye, leading to earlier detection of diseases such as cancer and improved patient outcomes (Esteva et al., 2019).

AI is also driving the rise of personalized medicine. By analyzing a patient's genetic information, medical history, and lifestyle factors, AI can help tailor treatments to individual needs. This shift from a one-size-fits-all approach to targeted, precision care increases treatment effectiveness while reducing side effects (Topol, 2019; WHO, 2021).

In predictive analytics, AI is helping identify patients at risk of chronic conditions such as diabetes or heart disease before symptoms appear. By recognizing patterns across millions of records, it enables proactive interventions that improve health outcomes and lower costs (OECD, 2023).

Beyond patient care, AI is optimizing healthcare operations – from scheduling and staffing to resource allocation and supply chain management. Hospitals are using AI to anticipate patient volumes, reduce wait times, and streamline administrative workflows. These efficiency gains allow providers to focus more on care delivery and less on paperwork (Ark Invest, 2021).

Overall, AI is enhancing both the clinical and operational aspects of healthcare. Its ability to process complex data at scale is helping clinicians make more informed decisions, accelerating medical research, and improving the patient experience. As the technology matures, AI will become an integral partner in delivering more intelligent, equitable, and efficient care.

References

- Ark Invest. 2021. *Big Ideas 2021: Artificial Intelligence.*
- Esteva, Andre, et al. 2019. "A Guide to Deep Learning in Healthcare." *Nature Medicine* 25 (1): 24–29.
- Organisation for Economic Co-operation and Development (OECD). 2023. *Artificial Intelligence in Health: The Future of Care Delivery.*
- Topol, Eric. 2019. *Deep Medicine: How Artificial Intelligence Can Make Healthcare Human Again.* Basic Books.

- World Health Organization (WHO). 2021. *Ethics and Governance of Artificial Intelligence for Health.*

4. DNA Sequencing

DNA sequencing is transforming healthcare by making personalized medicine a reality. It allows clinicians to analyze a patient's genetic makeup in unprecedented detail, offering insights that were once unattainable. This precision approach enables treatments tailored to individual patients, improving outcomes and reducing side effects (Topol, 2019).

In personalized medicine, DNA sequencing reveals how a person's genetic profile influences their response to specific treatments. This is particularly valuable in oncology, where sequencing can uncover mutations driving a patient's cancer. With this information, physicians can prescribe targeted therapies that directly address those genetic alterations, making treatment more effective and less toxic (NIH, 2020).

DNA sequencing also plays a crucial role in early detection. By examining a person's genome, clinicians can identify markers associated with an increased risk for conditions such as cancer, heart disease, or Alzheimer's. Detecting these risks early allows for preventative measures and close monitoring, improving the chances of early intervention and favorable outcomes (Collins et al., 2022).

Beyond diagnosis and treatment, sequencing helps identify inherited predispositions across families, guiding proactive lifestyle and medical decisions. For example, individuals with a BRCA1 or BRCA2 gene mutation may undergo regular screening or preventive care to reduce the likelihood of developing breast or ovarian cancer (National Human Genome Research Institute, 2023).

DNA sequencing is reshaping not just how diseases are treated, but how health itself is understood. By decoding the blueprint of life, healthcare can move toward truly individualized care – where prevention, diagnosis, and treatment are informed by the unique genetic profile of each person. This marks a fundamental shift toward more precise, predictive, and proactive medicine (Ark Invest, 2021).

References

- Ark Invest. 2021. *Big Ideas 2021: DNA Sequencing.*
- Collins, Francis S., M. Morgan, and A. Patrinos. 2022. "The Human Genome Project after 20 Years: Lessons, Impacts, and Future Perspectives." Nature 601 (7893): 38–45.
- National Human Genome Research Institute (NHGRI). 2023. *Genomics and Medicine: The Role of DNA Sequencing in Precision Healthcare.*
- National Institutes of Health (NIH). 2020. *Targeted Cancer Therapies.*
- Topol, Eric. 2019. *Deep Medicine: How Artificial Intelligence Can Make Healthcare Human Again. Basic Books.*

5. Energy Generation and Storage: Powering the Future of AI in Healthcare

Energy generation and storage are foundational to the integration and success of AI in healthcare. While often taken for granted, energy infrastructure underpins every modern AI-driven medical capability – from real-time diagnostics to robotic surgery. Reliable, resilient, and intelligent energy systems ensure that hospitals, clinics, and mobile health units can operate continuously, even in remote or unstable environments (IEA, 2023; WHO, 2022).

The Role of Energy Generation in Supporting AI Systems

AI systems require significant and consistent energy to function effectively. Continuous computation for diagnostics, patient monitoring, and predictive analytics demands uninterrupted power. Traditional energy grids alone are often insufficient, particularly in disaster-prone or rural regions. Healthcare providers are increasingly adopting **hybrid energy generation models** that combine renewable sources such as solar and wind with traditional power infrastructure.

AI itself plays a key role in optimizing this energy mix. Intelligent energy management platforms – like those developed by **Schneider Electric** – use predictive analytics to balance loads, forecast demand, and seamlessly switch between energy sources. These systems help hospitals maintain operational continuity while improving efficiency and lowering emissions (Schneider Electric, 2022).

Energy Storage: The Hidden Backbone of AI-Driven Care

Energy storage is as essential as generation. Without it, renewable power cannot deliver reliability. Advanced battery systems, such as **Tesla's Powerwall and Megapack** or **Fluence's grid-scale storage solutions**, store surplus energy and release it during outages or high-demand periods. In healthcare, this ensures that life-saving AI-powered technologies – ventilators, imaging systems, and robotic tools – continue operating during grid instability or natural disasters (Fluence, 2023; Tesla, 2023).

AI enhances this reliability further by predicting consumption patterns and managing discharge cycles, ensuring hospitals always have sufficient backup. This interplay between AI and energy storage creates a self-sustaining feedback loop: AI optimizes energy use, and reliable energy sustains AI-driven operations.

AI and Mobile Health: Energy Access in Remote Areas

Mobile health units equipped with AI-driven diagnostics are extending healthcare access to underserved regions. These units depend entirely on portable, renewable energy and compact storage systems. Innovations by companies such as **Goal Zero** enable clinics to operate independently of the grid, using solar generation and battery storage to power telemedicine, imaging, and diagnostic equipment. This democratization of care illustrates how energy innovation can make advanced healthcare universally accessible (Ark Invest, 2021).

Sustainability and the Energy-Intelligent Hospital

As hospitals digitize and expand AI use, energy demands are rising. Integrating renewables with AI-optimized storage reduces operational costs and environmental impact. **NextEra Energy** is pioneering solutions that combine renewable generation, AI analytics, and advanced battery systems, allowing hospitals to run more sustainably without compromising reliability (NextEra Energy, 2022).

Research published in *Nature Energy* highlights how AI algorithms can reduce overall energy waste in critical infrastructure, using dynamic forecasting to align energy production with demand (Nature Energy, 2021). These advances are transforming hospitals into energy-intelligent ecosystems – resilient, efficient, and sustainable.

The Future of AI-Enabled Healthcare Infrastructure

As AI becomes integral to healthcare, resilient energy systems will define the sector's future. Reliable power generation and intelligent storage ensure uninterrupted care delivery, no matter the setting. From hybrid hospital grids to portable solar-powered clinics, the integration of AI with energy infrastructure is not just an operational necessity – it's the foundation of equitable, sustainable healthcare for all.

In the end, energy doesn't just power hospitals – it powers the future of medicine.

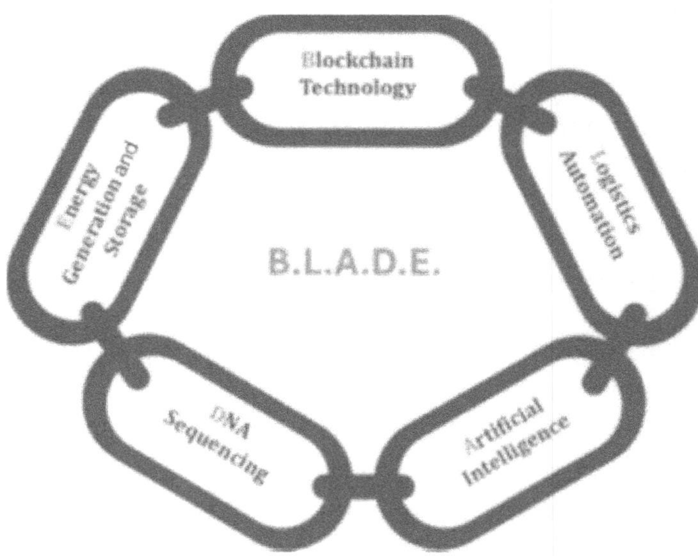

"The B.L.A.D.E. Framework: Five Convergent Layers of AI-Enabled Healthcare Infrastructure"

The B.L.A.D.E. framework – Blockchain, Logistics Automation, Artificial Intelligence, DNA Sequencing, and Energy – the five infrastructure pillars whose convergence defines 21st-century healthcare delivery.

References

- Ark Invest. 2021. *Big Ideas 2021: Energy Storage.*
- Fluence. 2023. *AI-Powered Grid Storage Solutions for Critical Infrastructure.*
- International Energy Agency (IEA). 2023. *World Energy Outlook 2023.*
- Nature Energy. 2021. "Artificial Intelligence and the Optimization of Energy Systems." Nature Energy 6 (7): 663–672.
- NextEra Energy. 2022. *AI and Energy Storage Integration in Sustainable Healthcare Facilities.*
- Schneider Electric. 2022. *AI-Driven Energy Management for Hospitals: Sustainability and Resilience.*
- Tesla. 2023. *Powering Hospitals with Tesla Energy: Powerwall and Megapack Applications.*
- World Health Organization (WHO). 2022. *Sustainable Energy Infrastructure for Health Facilities.*

The Interplay of These Five Transformative Technologies

Now, each of these technologies can and is by themselves poised to create a significant impact on healthcare. However, the seismic shift that is coming our way is really the convergence of these five – AI, robotics, energy storage, DNA sequencing, and blockchain technology. It's the convergence that is set to revolutionize healthcare. Here's how each pair of these technologies interplay to create this transformative potential.

1. AI and Robotics: A Powerful Synergy in Healthcare

AI and robotics are transforming healthcare by enhancing the precision and capabilities of medical procedures. This partnership combines the strengths of both technologies: AI processes and analyzes complex medical data, providing critical insights, while robotic systems execute these insights with unparalleled accuracy. The result is a more efficient healthcare system, particularly in surgical procedures, diagnostics, and rehabilitation.

A well-known example of this synergy is the Da Vinci Surgical System. It leverages AI to assist surgeons in performing minimally invasive procedures. AI's machine learning algorithms analyze patient data, guide robotic arms, and optimize each step of a surgery. This results in higher precision, fewer errors, and better patient outcomes, such as shorter recovery times and reduced complications.

Similar to the Da Vinci system, Vicarious Surgical is an emerging player in the AI and robotics space. Vicarious Surgical combines advanced robotics with AI-powered visualization and control systems to enhance the capabilities of surgeons. The company's technology uses virtual reality (VR) alongside robotics to offer surgeons a more immersive and precise view of the surgical field. AI-driven algorithms help automate certain aspects of surgery, such as cutting or suturing, reducing the physical burden on surgeons and increasing the accuracy of complex procedures.

This system interacts with AI by using real-time data analysis to adapt to the needs of each specific surgery. AI algorithms continuously monitor patient vitals, imaging data, and the robotic movements to ensure precise execution. This tight integration between AI and robotics allows for more flexible decision-making during surgery, and the ability to make micro-adjustments that enhance safety and efficiency.

How AI and Robotics Interact in Healthcare

The interaction between AI and robotics in healthcare isn't limited to providing more efficient surgeries. Their partnership affects multiple areas:

- **Pre-surgical planning:** AI systems analyze medical records, imaging scans, and patient data to help surgeons map out the best approach before even stepping into the operating room. By combining these insights with robotic precision, surgeons can carry out more effective procedures, reducing risks and optimizing outcomes.
- **Intraoperative precision:** During surgery, AI-powered robots can monitor real-time data – such as blood flow, tissue response, or pressure levels – and adjust movements accordingly. Robotic systems, guided by AI's continuous data analysis, can make micro-movements that would be impossible for a human hand to perform. This results in less invasive procedures, smaller incisions, and more precise targeting of affected areas.
- **Post-surgical recovery:** AI's ability to analyze a patient's progress after surgery, combined with robotic-assisted rehabilitation tools, helps speed up recovery. AI can tailor rehabilitation exercises based on real-time patient data, while robotics ensures precise execution of those exercises, aiding in quicker healing.

In these scenarios, AI and robotics feed off each other's strengths. AI processes vast amounts of data, providing predictive insights that enhance decision-making, while robotics performs the physical tasks with precision and consistency. This interaction allows for greater accuracy in surgeries and other medical procedures, translating to better patient outcomes.

Both Da Vinci and Vicarious Surgical show how the combination of AI and robotics is leading the charge in a new era of healthcare. These systems provide the tools to make surgeries safer, more efficient, and less invasive, while also improving recovery times and overall patient care. As AI continues to evolve, its ability to augment robotic systems will only deepen, paving the way for even more transformative healthcare innovations.

2. AI and DNA Sequencing

AI's ability to process and analyze large datasets is particularly beneficial for genomics. DNA sequencing generates massive amounts of data that require sophisticated algorithms to interpret. AI can identify genetic mutations and suggest personalized treatment plans based on a patient's genetic makeup, leading to more effective treatments and fewer adverse effects. AI's role in genomics is not just about data analysis; it's about creating actionable insights that can directly improve patient outcomes. For diseases like cancer, where treatment success often depends on an individual's genetic profile, AI-driven platforms have become invaluable. AI can process genomic data at incredible speeds, analyzing not only a patient's DNA but also how it interacts with their broader health history, lifestyle factors, and even treatment responses.

Example: Tempus is one of the leading companies in this field, combining AI with DNA sequencing to offer personalized cancer treatment recommendations. By analyzing a patient's genomic data, Tempus provides tailored insights to oncologists, helping them choose the most effective therapies while reducing side effects. This personalized approach to treatment has been shown to improve patient outcomes, especially in cases where standard treatments might not be effective due to the unique genetic characteristics of the tumor.

Another prominent player in this space is **Freenome**. Freenome uses a similar AI-driven approach but focuses on early detection and precision medicine, particularly in cancer screening. Their platform analyzes genetic markers and other biological signals to identify the early stages of cancer. Freenome's technology aims to detect cancer before symptoms appear, giving doctors more time to intervene with personalized treatment strategies. By using AI to process genomic and other biological data, Freenome provides a proactive approach to treatment, making early detection more accurate and accessible.

Companies like **Fabric Genomics** are also making strides by using AI to analyze whole-genome and exome sequencing data. Fabric Genomics provides tools for hospitals and research centers to integrate AI-driven insights into clinical workflows. This helps clinicians diagnose genetic disorders more quickly and with greater precision, allowing for targeted interventions that are based on a patient's entire genetic profile.

These companies demonstrate how AI and DNA sequencing are changing the landscape of personalized medicine. With the help of AI, genomic data can now be analyzed faster and more accurately than ever before. AI's ability to detect genetic mutations and patterns within massive datasets allows for individualized treatment plans that cater to the unique needs of each patient. In diseases like cancer, this means treatments can be fine-tuned to target specific genetic mutations, maximizing effectiveness while minimizing unnecessary side effects.

3. AI and Blockchain

Blockchain technology ensures secure and transparent data handling, which is crucial in healthcare where patient privacy is paramount. AI systems can leverage blockchain to access and analyze patient data securely, ensuring compliance with privacy regulations. For instance, AI algorithms can predict patient health trends using data stored on blockchain networks, ensuring data integrity and security.

Example: Companies like **Medicalchain** are using blockchain to secure patient data, which AI algorithms can then analyze to provide personalized health insights without compromising data privacy. Patients control who sees their medical information, ensuring transparency and privacy. AI algorithms can then use this data to generate personalized health insights or predict patient health trends, all while ensuring that the data remains secure and untampered. Another company making strides in this space is **BurstIQ**. BurstIQ uses blockchain to create secure, shareable health data profiles. These profiles enable AI systems to analyze a patient's data without risking privacy or security. BurstIQ's platform is designed to facilitate data sharing between healthcare providers, researchers, and patients while maintaining compliance with privacy regulations like HIPAA. AI can then work within this secure framework to deliver predictive analytics, personalized treatment plans, or even identify public health trends across populations.

Both Medicalchain and BurstIQ exemplify how blockchain and cryptography are enhancing healthcare's ability to leverage AI without compromising patient privacy. Blockchain ensures that data remains secure and verifiable, while AI uses that data to transform healthcare delivery. Together, they allow for the creation of personalized treatments, predictive health models, and more efficient healthcare systems, all while maintaining the integrity and privacy of sensitive health information.

4. AI and Energy Generation/Storage: Powering the Future of Healthcare

AI is rapidly transforming healthcare, but one often overlooked factor in this transformation is the energy required to power these advanced systems. AI-driven healthcare requires a constant, reliable supply of energy to ensure that life-saving technologies, critical medical devices, and hospital systems function without interruption. This is where the integration of AI with energy generation and storage becomes crucial – not just to optimize energy use, but also to ensure that AI technologies are accessible and cost-effective in healthcare facilities everywhere.

The Need for Additional Energy Generation

As healthcare facilities increasingly adopt AI systems for diagnostics, robotics, and patient monitoring, their energy demands are growing. AI algorithms process massive datasets and operate continuously to deliver real-time insights. This requires significant computational power, which, in turn, places more pressure on primary energy sources. Traditional energy grids often struggle to meet this demand, especially in facilities located in remote or disaster-prone areas. To support the needs of AI-driven healthcare, facilities need not only stable energy but also additional primary sources of energy, such as solar or wind.

For example, companies like NextEra Energy are focusing on integrating renewable energy generation with AI systems to ensure that hospitals and clinics can access cleaner, more sustainable power sources. By analyzing energy usage patterns and predicting future demand, AI can help healthcare facilities decide when to switch from traditional grid power to renewable energy, ensuring that critical devices remain operational without disruption. In a hospital setting, where even a momentary lapse in energy can be catastrophic, such smart energy management systems play a pivotal role.

The Role of Energy Storage

While AI can help manage primary energy generation, it also plays a vital role in energy storage. The energy needs of healthcare facilities don't stop when the sun goes down or the wind stops blowing. This is where AI-driven energy storage solutions become essential, making sure that hospitals and medical centers have uninterrupted power at all times. Energy storage systems, such as battery backups, must be intelligently managed to store excess energy when demand is low and release it when needed, especially during peak times or emergencies.

Companies like Tesla, through their Powerwall and Powerpack products, provide AI-optimized battery storage solutions for healthcare facilities. These energy storage systems are designed to store surplus renewable energy and automatically kick in during grid failures or shortages. AI algorithms continuously monitor energy consumption and predict when stored energy will be needed, ensuring that life-saving equipment like ventilators, heart monitors, and surgical robots can continue functioning even during power outages.

Meanwhile, Fluence, a leader in energy storage technology, is deploying AI-driven platforms that optimize the use of large-scale battery systems in hospitals. Fluence's AI systems analyze real-time data on energy use and grid stability, ensuring that backup power sources are activated at the precise moment they are needed. This approach reduces energy waste and ensures that hospitals can rely on consistent, efficient power – even in situations where the primary energy grid is down or under strain.

The Interaction between AI and Energy Storage

AI's ability to manage energy storage systems goes beyond simply switching between primary and secondary power sources. It ensures energy efficiency by predicting energy demand and controlling how and when stored energy is used. In a hospital, this might mean that less critical systems are temporarily powered down to reserve energy for essential devices like incubators, surgical robots, or AI-driven diagnostic machines. AI optimizes energy usage to maintain continuous operation while reducing costs, making cutting-edge healthcare technology more accessible even in resource-limited settings.

Moreover, as healthcare systems become more reliant on telemedicine and portable medical devices, particularly in remote or rural areas, energy storage becomes a critical factor in making these AI-driven tools available anywhere. AI-driven energy storage systems make it possible for mobile health units or clinics to operate in areas where reliable grid power is scarce or non-existent. For instance, Tesla's Powerpack system combined with AI allows healthcare facilities in such regions to store solar energy and use it at night or during emergencies, ensuring that diagnostic machines, patient monitoring systems, and AI-powered equipment are always operational.

Why This Matters

Without reliable energy storage solutions, the potential for AI in healthcare would be significantly limited. AI systems cannot function without constant power, and healthcare facilities that struggle with unreliable energy sources cannot fully benefit from the advanced capabilities AI offers, from real-time monitoring to life-saving surgical robots. Additionally, AI's ability to manage energy usage and storage makes it possible for healthcare providers to reduce costs, making these technologies more scalable and accessible to a broader population.

The synergy between AI and energy storage isn't just about ensuring consistent power – it's about making AI-driven healthcare available and affordable in more places. As companies like NextEra, Tesla, and Fluence continue to push the boundaries of energy management and storage, healthcare systems will become more resilient, sustainable, and capable of meeting the growing demands placed on them by AI technologies.

In short, AI and energy storage together form the backbone of the next generation of healthcare, ensuring that critical technologies can operate anywhere, anytime, at a lower cost. This integration is vital for the future of healthcare, particularly as AI becomes more deeply embedded in medical practices around the world.

5. Robotics and DNA Sequencing: Driving Precision and Efficiency in Healthcare

The combination of robotics and DNA sequencing is rapidly advancing personalized medicine and genomics. While DNA sequencing has already transformed the way we understand and treat disease, the integration of robotics automates and accelerates this process, allowing for faster, more accurate genetic analysis. In healthcare, where time and precision are critical, robotics not only enhances the efficiency of sequencing but also ensures the consistency and reliability needed to bring precision medicine to the forefront.

Robotics has a unique ability to automate the complex, repetitive, and precise tasks required in DNA sequencing, which traditionally rely on manual labor. By leveraging robotics, healthcare facilities and research labs can process massive amounts of genetic data at speeds unattainable by human hands, reducing errors and freeing up healthcare professionals to focus on higher-level tasks.

Why Robotics and DNA Sequencing Matter for Healthcare

DNA sequencing generates vast amounts of data, especially when applied to whole genomes. This data is the foundation of personalized medicine, where treatments can be tailored to a patient's specific genetic profile. However, manual sequencing processes are slow, labor-intensive, and prone to errors, which limits the potential for widespread adoption in clinical settings.

Robotics addresses these challenges by automating every stage of the sequencing process, from sample preparation to data analysis. Automation not only increases throughput, allowing laboratories to sequence more samples in less time, but also reduces human error, ensuring more accurate results. The faster and more accurately genetic data can be processed, the quicker patients can receive personalized treatments, improving outcomes and reducing the risk of adverse reactions to therapies.

This intersection between robotics and DNA sequencing is particularly important in areas like oncology, where time-sensitive genetic information can guide critical treatment decisions. For example, identifying mutations in a cancer patient's tumor can help oncologists select therapies that target those specific mutations, dramatically increasing the chances of treatment success.

Examples of Companies Already Driving Innovation in Robotics and DNA Sequencing

Illumina

Illumina is a pioneer in the DNA sequencing industry, known for its cutting-edge sequencing technology. The company has incorporated robotics to automate many of the repetitive tasks involved in sequencing. By integrating robotics into their Next Generation Sequencing (NGS) platforms, Illumina has significantly increased throughput while lowering costs, making genomic analysis more accessible and scalable. Their automated systems allow for rapid, high-accuracy sequencing of DNA, which accelerates research and clinical diagnostics. For example, in oncology, Illumina's robotic systems can sequence tumor DNA more quickly, enabling faster turnaround for personalized cancer treatment plans.

Thermo Fisher Scientific

Thermo Fisher Scientific is another leader at the intersection of robotics and DNA sequencing. Their Ion Torrent sequencing platform is designed with automated sample preparation systems that streamline the entire workflow, reducing the time from sample to result. Thermo Fisher's use of robotics minimizes manual interventions, leading to higher precision in sequencing, which is critical for applications such as genetic disorder diagnosis or pharmacogenomics. By automating sequencing workflows, Thermo Fisher ensures that healthcare providers can deliver personalized treatments more quickly, improving patient outcomes and reducing time spent on trial-and-error therapies.

Hamilton Robotics

Hamilton Robotics is a key player in lab automation and has developed robotic systems specifically designed for high-throughput DNA sequencing workflows. Their Microlab STAR system automates the liquid handling and sample preparation stages of DNA sequencing, significantly increasing the speed and consistency of genetic analysis. Hamilton's robotics are designed to work in tandem with sequencing platforms, improving accuracy while reducing the manual labor required in sequencing. In clinical labs and research centers, Hamilton's systems allow for the processing of thousands of DNA samples simultaneously, driving faster insights in genomics and personalized medicine.

The Impact on Healthcare

For patients, the marriage of robotics and DNA sequencing means faster diagnoses and treatments. Consider a patient with a rare genetic disorder: traditionally, it might take weeks or even months to sequence the patient's DNA and identify the genetic mutation responsible for the condition. With robotic automation, this process can be completed in days, allowing for quicker diagnosis and more rapid development of a personalized treatment plan.

In oncology, where genetic sequencing of tumors is essential for determining the most effective treatment, robotics accelerates the time it takes to sequence a tumor's DNA, analyze the mutations, and provide actionable insights for oncologists. This speed can make the difference between a timely, life-saving intervention and a delayed or less effective treatment.

Furthermore, this synergy between robotics and DNA sequencing is critical for public health, especially in times of crisis. During the COVID-19 pandemic, rapid genomic sequencing of the virus was crucial for tracking mutations and developing vaccines. Robotic systems played an essential role in processing large numbers of viral samples, allowing researchers to map the virus's genetic changes quickly and efficiently.

Why It Matters to You

If you're a healthcare provider, administrator, or patient, the integration of robotics and DNA sequencing affects you directly. For healthcare professionals, it means faster, more reliable tools to diagnose and treat patients with genetic diseases. For administrators, it means greater efficiency, lower costs, and the ability to scale genetic testing capabilities across entire healthcare systems. For patients, this technology enables access to treatments that are specifically tailored to your genetic profile, offering better outcomes with fewer side effects.

The continued evolution of robotics and DNA sequencing will further democratize access to genomic medicine, making it a routine part of healthcare rather than a niche service available only to a few. As companies like Illumina, Thermo Fisher Scientific, and Hamilton Robotics continue to innovate, the benefits of personalized medicine will become more widespread, offering hope to millions of patients who stand to benefit from faster, more effective treatments.

In short, the intersection of robotics and DNA sequencing is not just about making healthcare more efficient – it's about making healthcare smarter, more precise, and more personalized for every patient.

6. Robotics and Blockchain: Enhancing Security and Transparency in Healthcare

As healthcare technology continues to evolve, the integration of robotics and blockchain is emerging as a powerful force for improving patient care. Robotics already plays a transformative role in surgery, rehabilitation, and patient monitoring, offering precision and efficiency that were previously unattainable. However, as these systems collect and process vast amounts of sensitive data, ensuring the security, integrity, and transparency of this data becomes crucial. That's where blockchain technology comes in.

Blockchain, with its decentralized and immutable structure, can provide a secure and transparent way to manage and audit the data generated by robotic systems in healthcare. By combining the precision of robotics with the transparency and security of blockchain, healthcare providers can enhance accountability, improve patient safety, and build trust in the increasing role of automation in medical care.

Why Robotics and Blockchain Matter for Healthcare

In healthcare, **data security and accountability** are critical. As robotic systems become more advanced, performing tasks from minimally invasive surgeries to automated patient monitoring, they generate a vast amount of data. This includes not only patient information but also detailed logs of the actions performed by the robots themselves. Ensuring that this data remains secure, tamper-proof, and accessible to the right people – while still complying with privacy regulations like HIPAA – requires robust systems that go beyond traditional data management solutions.

Blockchain technology addresses these concerns by providing a decentralized ledger that records every action and piece of data generated by robotic systems in real time. These records are immutable, meaning they cannot be altered retroactively, which ensures full transparency and accountability. In critical areas like robotic surgery or automated medication dispensing, this transparency builds trust among patients, healthcare providers, and regulators by ensuring that every step of the process is securely documented and verifiable.

Examples of Companies Already Innovating at the Intersection of Robotics and Blockchain

1. **ProvenMed**
   – **ProvenMed** is pioneering the integration of robotics and blockchain in healthcare, particularly in urology. The company developed a medical device called the **ActivGo** system, a wearable robotic device designed to assist patients with urinary disorders. ProvenMed is exploring blockchain to securely store patient data collected by this robotic system, ensuring that all interactions between the device and the patient are logged in an immutable ledger.

This level of data integrity and transparency ensures that healthcare providers can track device usage and patient outcomes securely, with full accountability. Blockchain provides an additional layer of trust, ensuring that the data generated by the robotic device is accurate, traceable, and compliant with privacy laws.

2. **Vicarious Surgical**
   - **Vicarious Surgical**, a company at the forefront of robotic-assisted surgery, is exploring blockchain to enhance the security and auditability of surgical data. Their robotic systems, which provide surgeons with high-precision, minimally invasive surgical tools, generate detailed logs of every action taken during a procedure. By integrating blockchain, Vicarious Surgical aims to ensure that these logs are not only secure but also auditable by both healthcare providers and regulators. Blockchain can serve as an immutable record of each surgery, providing full transparency and accountability for every procedure performed. This level of trust is crucial as robotic-assisted surgeries become more common, ensuring that both patients and healthcare providers have access to a verifiable record of every step taken during a procedure.
3. **Skychain**
   - **Skychain** is a blockchain-powered AI platform designed for healthcare, but it's also exploring the integration of robotic systems. By using blockchain to log the data generated by robots in diagnostic and treatment scenarios, Skychain ensures that healthcare providers can securely access and verify this information. In combination with AI, Skychain's platform provides transparency over robotic interactions, reducing the potential for errors and increasing trust in automated systems. Skychain's focus on secure data sharing among

healthcare providers, patients, and insurers makes it an ideal candidate for further integrating robotic data into a transparent and auditable system.

The Interaction between Robotics and Blockchain in Healthcare

The collaboration between robotics and blockchain addresses two critical needs in healthcare: **security** and **transparency**. Robotic systems, whether used in surgeries, diagnostics, or patient care, are becoming increasingly sophisticated, generating detailed records of every task they perform. Blockchain ensures that these records are securely stored in a decentralized ledger, protecting them from tampering or unauthorized access.

In robotic surgeries, for example, blockchain can serve as an auditable trail of every action taken during the procedure. If there's a need to review the surgery later – whether to evaluate outcomes, investigate complications, or provide legal documentation – healthcare providers and regulators can rely on the blockchain record to offer an immutable, transparent view of the procedure. This level of accountability is particularly important as the use of robotics in surgery becomes more widespread, and the need for verifiable data becomes more urgent.

Blockchain also facilitates **secure data sharing**. For instance, in a scenario where multiple healthcare providers need access to data generated by robotic systems, blockchain ensures that this data is shared securely, with full transparency over who has accessed the information and for what purpose. This is especially important for maintaining compliance with regulations like HIPAA, as blockchain's encryption ensures that patient data remains secure while still accessible to authorized parties.

Why This Should Matter to You

If you are a healthcare provider, administrator, or patient, the intersection of robotics and blockchain impacts the security and reliability of the care you provide or receive. For healthcare professionals, blockchain ensures that the data generated by robotic systems is accurate, tamper-proof, and easily auditable. This not only improves patient safety but also builds trust in the growing role of automation in healthcare.

For patients, blockchain offers reassurance that their data is secure and that the actions performed by robotic systems – whether during surgery or in routine patient care – are recorded transparently. It adds a layer of accountability that ensures healthcare providers can track and verify every step of the care process.

7. Robotics and Energy Storage: Ensuring Continuous Operation in Healthcare

Robotics is revolutionizing healthcare, from robotic-assisted surgeries to automated patient monitoring systems, but these technologies depend on reliable and efficient energy sources. The advanced capabilities of robotic systems require continuous power to ensure precision, safety, and functionality. This need becomes even more critical in healthcare environments where any power disruption could endanger lives. For instance, during complex surgeries or in critical care units, interruptions in robotic system operations can lead to severe complications.

This is where **energy storage** solutions come into play. Advances in high-capacity batteries and energy storage technologies are making it possible for healthcare facilities to ensure uninterrupted robotic operations, even in challenging environments. Whether it's in remote areas with limited infrastructure or in urban hospitals experiencing power fluctuations, robust energy storage systems provide the reliable power needed to keep these essential healthcare robots functioning.

Why Robotics and Energy Storage Matter for Healthcare

Healthcare facilities depend heavily on the continuous operation of robotic systems to perform critical tasks. Robotic surgery platforms, for example, assist surgeons in performing delicate, minimally invasive procedures that require absolute precision. Similarly, robotic systems in patient monitoring provide real-time data on vital signs, allowing healthcare providers to respond quickly to changes in a patient's condition. Any disruption to these systems can lead to delayed treatments, increased risk to patients, and a breakdown in overall care.

Reliable energy storage is critical in ensuring that robotic systems can operate without interruption, particularly in times of power outages, natural disasters, or in regions with an unreliable energy grid. High-capacity batteries, combined with AI-optimized energy management, ensure that hospitals can continue operating their robotic systems even during blackouts or infrastructure failures. This technology not only supports uninterrupted medical care but also ensures that hospitals are more resilient in the face of emergencies.

Leading Companies Driving Innovation at the Intersection of Robotics and Energy Storage

1. **Medtronic**
   - **Medtronic**, a global leader in medical technology, is integrating advanced energy storage solutions into its robotic platforms. Their **Hugo™ RAS**

(robotic-assisted surgery) system relies on continuous power to ensure precision during minimally invasive surgeries. Medtronic is working with energy storage providers to incorporate high-capacity, long-lasting batteries into their systems, ensuring the Hugo RAS system can continue operating even during unexpected power interruptions. This integration of energy storage is crucial for maintaining the system's reliability in both well-equipped urban hospitals and in more remote healthcare settings where the power grid may be less stable.

2. **ABB**
   - **ABB**, a leader in robotics and automation technologies, is also innovating in the healthcare space by developing robotics with integrated energy storage solutions. ABB's robotics are used in a variety of healthcare applications, including patient handling, laboratory automation, and even robotic surgery. Through its partnerships with battery technology companies, ABB ensures that its healthcare robots are equipped with energy-efficient power systems. In regions with unreliable power infrastructure, ABB's solutions provide healthcare facilities with autonomous, battery-powered robots that can function for extended periods without needing to rely on the grid. This is especially important in disaster-stricken or remote areas, where robotics can ensure continuous care even when the local power supply is disrupted.
3. **Tesla**
   - **Tesla**, known for its innovations in electric vehicles and energy storage, is making strides in healthcare by providing advanced **Powerwall** and **Powerpack** solutions that can power entire hospitals or mobile health units. While Tesla is not directly developing medical robotics, its energy

storage technology is critical for healthcare facilities that rely on robotic systems. Tesla's batteries store energy from renewable sources like solar power, ensuring that hospitals have a reliable, green power supply. In remote healthcare units, where access to a stable grid is limited, Tesla's Powerpack systems ensure that robots used for surgery, patient care, or diagnostics can continue to function without interruption, enhancing both reliability and sustainability.

The Interaction between Robotics and Energy Storage in Healthcare

The relationship between robotics and energy storage is vital in ensuring the success of **robotic-assisted healthcare**. Robotic systems, whether they are used in surgical procedures, patient monitoring, or in mobile healthcare units, require a constant power supply to ensure seamless operation. However, in areas where power supply is inconsistent – such as rural regions, disaster-stricken zones, or even urban hospitals with aging infrastructure – this continuity can be a challenge.

Energy storage systems, particularly **high-capacity batteries**, solve this issue by storing excess energy that can be used when the primary power supply is disrupted. These systems are capable of powering robotic units during surgery, patient care, or diagnostics without the risk of failure due to power outages. In addition, advanced energy storage technologies like **Tesla's Powerwall** or **ABB's integrated power solutions** ensure that robotic systems can be deployed in remote locations or emergency situations where consistent access to the power grid may not be guaranteed.

Robotics paired with energy storage also facilitates **mobile healthcare units**, which are increasingly used to provide medical services in underserved areas. These units often rely on AI-driven robotic tools for diagnostics or patient care. Without advanced energy storage, these units would not be able to operate autonomously for long periods. With the ability to store and use renewable energy, mobile health units equipped with robotics can function in even the most remote environments, providing life-saving care in regions where traditional healthcare infrastructure is lacking.

Why This Should Matter to You

For healthcare providers, administrators, and patients alike, the integration of robotics and energy storage represents a significant step forward in ensuring the **reliability and resilience** of healthcare systems. For hospitals and clinics, investing in robotics without addressing power reliability risks undermining the very benefits that robotics brings – precision, efficiency, and uninterrupted care. Energy storage ensures that these investments in technology can deliver their full value, even during power disruptions or in areas where grid infrastructure is unreliable.

For healthcare professionals, energy storage paired with robotics ensures that critical operations, such as robotic surgeries or automated monitoring systems, continue uninterrupted. This reduces the risk of medical errors caused by power failures, enhances patient outcomes, and provides a more stable environment for both medical professionals and patients.

For patients, particularly those in remote or underserved areas, the combination of robotics and energy storage in mobile healthcare units brings cutting-edge care directly to them. Whether it's a telemedicine consultation powered by autonomous robots or life-saving surgeries performed in a mobile unit, reliable energy storage ensures that advanced healthcare is not limited by location or infrastructure constraints.

The Future of Robotics and Energy Storage in Healthcare

As companies like **Medtronic**, **ABB**, and **Tesla** continue to innovate at the intersection of robotics and energy storage, healthcare facilities will become more resilient, efficient, and capable of delivering continuous, high-quality care. The integration of these technologies is essential for ensuring that robotic systems can operate effectively, especially in challenging environments where power supply is unreliable.

Looking ahead, this intersection will only grow more critical as robotics and automation become more widespread in healthcare. The combination of **energy storage and robotics** is not just about enhancing current capabilities – it's about future-proofing healthcare for the inevitable challenges of tomorrow. Whether through robotic-assisted surgeries, AI-driven diagnostics, or remote healthcare delivery, the synergy between robotics and energy storage will ensure that healthcare remains reliable, accessible, and effective for all.

8. DNA Sequencing and Blockchain: Securing the Future of Genomic Data in Healthcare

DNA sequencing is rapidly becoming a cornerstone of personalized medicine, offering detailed insights into a patient's genetic makeup that can drive highly specific and effective treatments. However, as the amount of genetic data grows, so do concerns about privacy, security, and data sharing. The sensitivity of genomic data makes it a prime target for misuse if not properly protected. This is where **blockchain technology** plays a crucial role, providing a secure, decentralized, and tamper-proof method for storing and sharing genetic information.

Blockchain ensures that the results of DNA sequencing are accessible to authorized parties – such as healthcare providers and researchers – without compromising privacy. By maintaining the integrity and security of genomic data, blockchain technology supports the safe advancement of personalized medicine, allowing AI and other technologies to analyze genetic information while adhering to strict privacy regulations. This combination is especially important as genetic data becomes more valuable in predicting disease, creating targeted treatments, and advancing medical research.

Why DNA Sequencing and Blockchain Matter for Healthcare

As genomic sequencing becomes more prevalent in healthcare, the need for a **secure and transparent system** to store, access, and share genetic data is paramount. DNA sequencing generates highly sensitive information about an individual's genetic predispositions, disease risks, and potential responses to treatments. Mishandling or unauthorized access to this data could have serious ethical and legal implications, not to mention privacy concerns for patients.

Blockchain technology addresses these concerns by creating an immutable, decentralized ledger where every transaction involving genetic data is securely recorded. This ensures that only authorized individuals or organizations can access and modify genetic information, reducing the risk of data breaches. Blockchain also gives patients greater control over their own genomic data, enabling them to decide who can access their information and for what purpose. This added layer of security is critical for building trust in personalized medicine, where data privacy is just as important as the treatments themselves.

Moreover, blockchain's transparency ensures that every action – whether it's data access, modification, or sharing – can be traced and audited. This capability enhances trust between patients, healthcare providers, and researchers, as all parties can verify that the data has not been tampered with and is being used appropriately.

Leading Companies at the Intersection of DNA Sequencing and Blockchain

1. **Nebula Genomics**
   - **Nebula Genomics** is a leader in integrating DNA sequencing with blockchain technology to give patients complete control over their genetic data. Nebula allows individuals to have their entire genome sequenced and then securely store the results using blockchain technology. Patients can choose to share their genetic information with healthcare providers or researchers on a case-by-case basis. Each transaction is logged on a blockchain, ensuring that the data is only accessed by authorized individuals and is not altered without permission. This system provides an unprecedented level of transparency and control for patients, ensuring privacy while also contributing to medical research aimed at advancing personalized treatments.
2. **EncrypGen**
   - **EncrypGen** offers a platform called **Gene-Chain**, which enables the secure sharing and storage of genetic data using blockchain. EncrypGen's platform

allows users to upload their DNA sequencing data into a decentralized database, where it can be securely accessed by researchers, clinicians, or pharmaceutical companies. EncrypGen also offers a marketplace where individuals can share their genomic data with researchers in exchange for compensation. Blockchain ensures that all transactions are transparent and that the data remains secure. EncrypGen's use of blockchain allows for the creation of a decentralized repository of genetic data, which could significantly accelerate advancements in personalized medicine by providing researchers with secure, reliable access to large datasets.

3. **Zenome**
   - **Zenome** is another key player in the DNA sequencing and blockchain space. The **Zenome platform** offers users the ability to sequence their DNA and store it securely on a blockchain. Zenome emphasizes patient control, allowing users to decide who can access their genetic information and how it will be used. Through its blockchain-based marketplace, individuals can share their data with healthcare providers or researchers while maintaining full transparency over every interaction. Zenome's model prioritizes patient privacy and autonomy, creating a secure ecosystem where genetic data can be used to drive advancements in personalized medicine without compromising individual rights.

The Interaction between DNA Sequencing and Blockchain in Healthcare

Blockchain's **decentralized structure** is essential for ensuring the privacy and security of genomic data. DNA sequencing reveals deeply personal information about a person's health risks and genetic traits, so its handling requires the highest levels of security. With blockchain, every action related to genetic data – whether it's storage, access, or sharing – is recorded in an immutable ledger. This means that once a piece of data is entered into the blockchain, it cannot be altered without leaving a clear and auditable trail.

For healthcare providers, this interaction between DNA sequencing and blockchain technology means they can securely access patients' genetic data to create personalized treatment plans. In the realm of **personalized medicine**, the ability to safely and reliably share genetic information across different providers and institutions is crucial. Blockchain facilitates this process by ensuring that the data being shared is both accurate and secure.

Furthermore, blockchain empowers patients to **take control** of their own genetic information. In traditional healthcare systems, data is often stored by the healthcare provider, leaving patients with little control over how their data is used. Blockchain reverses this dynamic by giving patients the ability to grant or revoke access to their genetic information in real time. This transparency builds trust between patients and healthcare providers, which is essential as more patients undergo genetic testing to guide their treatment plans.

The combination of **AI, DNA sequencing, and blockchain** also opens up new possibilities for medical research. Blockchain can serve as a secure platform for researchers to access vast, anonymized genetic datasets without risking patient privacy. By analyzing this data, AI systems can uncover patterns that lead to the development of more targeted treatments for various diseases, particularly in oncology, cardiology, and rare genetic disorders.

Why This Should Matter to You

For patients, healthcare providers, and researchers, the integration of DNA sequencing and blockchain is a

game-changer in the realm of personalized medicine. If you are a healthcare professional, blockchain ensures that you can access and use genetic data securely and responsibly, improving the quality of care you provide. For administrators, blockchain technology can reduce the risks of data breaches and ensure compliance with stringent data privacy regulations, creating a more trustworthy and transparent healthcare environment.

As a patient, this technology matters because it gives you **greater control** over your most sensitive health information. With blockchain, you can decide who has access to your genetic data and track how it's being used. This empowers you to participate in your own healthcare journey while knowing that your privacy is protected.

Finally, for researchers and pharmaceutical companies, blockchain's decentralized databases allow for secure access to a wealth of genetic data, helping to accelerate **innovations in drug development and personalized therapies**. By maintaining data integrity and privacy, blockchain enables the use of genomic data on a scale that was previously impossible, creating opportunities for breakthroughs in treatment and diagnosis.

The Future of DNA Sequencing and Blockchain in Healthcare

As companies like **Nebula Genomics**, **EncrypGen**, and **Zenome** continue to push the boundaries of what is possible at the intersection of DNA sequencing and blockchain, healthcare is becoming more secure, transparent, and patient-centered. The ability to store, access, and share genetic data securely is not just a technological advancement – it's a **necessary evolution** in modern medicine, ensuring that the next generation of treatments is built on trust, transparency, and privacy.

In the future, the integration of blockchain and DNA sequencing will be essential for advancing personalized medicine, enabling patients and providers to collaborate in new ways and ensuring that sensitive genetic data is always handled with the highest levels of security. The **decentralization of genomic data** will play a pivotal role in unlocking the full potential of AI in healthcare, driving the creation of personalized treatments that improve outcomes and save lives.

9. DNA Sequencing and Energy Storage: Powering Genomic Research and Clinical Diagnostics

DNA sequencing has revolutionized healthcare by enabling precision medicine, offering detailed insights into a patient's genetic makeup that guide personalized treatments. However, the high-tech equipment required for DNA sequencing is energy-intensive and must operate continuously to ensure the accuracy of both research and clinical diagnostics. Any interruption in power can jeopardize the integrity of the data being collected, potentially leading to delays or errors in patient care or genomic research.

This is where **energy storage solutions** come into play. High-capacity, reliable, and sustainable energy storage systems ensure that DNA sequencing machines operate without interruption, even in regions where power supply may be inconsistent or unreliable. Whether in a cutting-edge research lab or a hospital in a remote area, these energy storage technologies provide the necessary power to keep sequencing machines running smoothly, safeguarding the integrity of the data and enabling healthcare professionals to deliver accurate and timely results.

Why DNA Sequencing and Energy Storage Matter for Healthcare

As DNA sequencing becomes an integral part of healthcare, from **genomic research** to **clinical diagnostics**, the need for a reliable power supply grows. DNA sequencing machines run complex algorithms and require significant computational power to analyze vast amounts of genetic data. A sudden power outage during a sequencing process can not only delay research and diagnostics but also compromise the integrity of the data, leading to inaccurate results or the need to rerun costly and time-consuming tests.

Energy storage systems, such as **advanced batteries** and **backup power solutions**, mitigate these risks by ensuring that DNA sequencing machines have a stable power supply. This is particularly important in areas with unstable power grids or in laboratories and clinics that rely on renewable energy sources, which may fluctuate. With the right energy storage solutions in place, these facilities can ensure continuous operation, protecting the accuracy of genomic data and enabling more efficient healthcare delivery.

Leading Companies Driving Innovation at the Intersection of DNA Sequencing and Energy Storage

1. **Pacific Biosciences (PacBio)**
   - **PacBio** is a leader in the DNA sequencing field, known for its highly accurate long-read sequencing technology. The company's sequencing platforms require continuous, stable power to perform complex analyses of genetic data. To address the energy demands of their systems, PacBio integrates advanced energy storage solutions in its equipment. This ensures that sequencing can continue uninterrupted, even in regions with unreliable power. PacBio's ability to maintain the continuous operation of its machines is essential for both cutting-edge genomic research and clinical applications, where any delay or interruption could compromise the results.

2. **Tesla**
   – While primarily known for its electric vehicles, **Tesla** is also a leader in energy storage solutions, which are increasingly being adopted in healthcare environments. Tesla's **Powerpack** and **Powerwall** systems provide high-capacity, long-lasting energy storage that ensures uninterrupted power for DNA sequencing labs and clinics. These systems store excess energy generated from renewable sources or grid power, ensuring a constant energy supply for sequencing equipment. In remote areas or regions with unreliable electricity grids, Tesla's energy storage solutions allow hospitals and research centers to continue their work without disruption, enhancing the reliability of genomic testing and research.
3. **Illumina**
   – **Illumina**, one of the most prominent companies in the DNA sequencing space, produces platforms that are widely used in both clinical and research settings. The high-energy demands of Illumina's machines have led the company to invest in energy storage solutions to ensure seamless operation. Illumina's sequencing platforms often operate in diverse environments, from state-of-the-art research centers to mobile labs in remote locations. With energy storage systems providing backup power, Illumina's equipment can run continuously, ensuring that genetic data is processed accurately and on time. This reliability is essential for the growing field of personalized medicine, where sequencing data is used to develop individualized treatment plans.

The Interaction between DNA Sequencing and Energy Storage in Healthcare

The integration of **energy storage** with DNA sequencing equipment is critical to maintaining the continuous operation that genomic research and clinical diagnostics require. DNA sequencing involves highly complex, long-running processes that can take hours or even days to complete. Any power disruption can result in the loss of valuable data, costly delays, or the need to restart the sequencing process. This is especially problematic in clinical settings where sequencing results are needed quickly to guide critical treatment decisions.

By incorporating advanced energy storage systems, healthcare facilities and research labs can safeguard their sequencing operations against power fluctuations or outages. These storage systems are capable of powering sequencing machines for extended periods during outages, ensuring that operations remain smooth and data integrity is preserved. In regions with unreliable electricity grids, energy storage allows DNA sequencing to continue without disruption, enabling healthcare providers to deliver precise and timely diagnostics, even in challenging conditions.

For example, in remote areas where **mobile health units** or small clinics rely on solar power, energy storage systems like Tesla's Powerpack can store excess energy generated during the day and provide power overnight or during cloudy conditions. This capability ensures that DNA sequencing machines can operate continuously, giving healthcare providers the tools they need to analyze genetic data and deliver personalized care, regardless of geographic location.

Additionally, the role of **sustainability** in healthcare is becoming increasingly important. As hospitals and research labs transition to renewable energy sources, energy storage solutions ensure that the variability of solar or wind power doesn't disrupt critical operations like DNA sequencing. With the help of energy storage, healthcare facilities can reduce their environmental impact while maintaining the reliability of their genomic diagnostics and research.

Interaction Between DNA Sequencing and Global Energy (Electricity) Availability

Year	Cost per Genome (USD)	Global Electricity Generation (TWh)	Data Type	Notes / Sources
2010	$ 50,000.00	21600	Observed	NHGRI / OWID cost series (−99.9 % since 2001); OWID Electricity Generation dataset (IEA/EI/Ember).
2011	$ 10,000.00	22100	Observed	Rapid drop after Illumina HiSeq launch; global generation rising ≈ 2.3 %.
2012	$ 7,000.00	22700	Observed	NHGRI cost data; early massive parallel sequencing adoption.
2013	$ 5,000.00	23300	Observed	Introduction of Illumina NextSeq platforms.
2014	$ 4,000.00	23800	Observed	Steady cost decline; renewable generation ≈ 23 % of total.
2015	$ 1,500.00	24000	Observed	First sub-$2 000 human genome.
2016	$ 1,300.00	24800	Observed	Cost plateau begins; IEA reports ~3 % electricity growth.
2017	$ 1,000.00	25700	Observed	Automation and cloud genomics expansion.
2018	$ 950.00	26700	Observed	NHGRI records flattening; renewables share continues climb.
2019	$ 700.00	27000	Observed	Large-scale population genomics projects start.
2020	$ 600.00	26800	Observed	Pandemic dip in electric demand.
2021	$ 560.00	27800	Observed	Post-pandemic rebound; record solar additions.
2022	$ 525.00	28500	Observed	NHGRI last official value (2022 update).
2023	$ 525.00	29300	Observed / proxy	Carry-forward cost; OWID 2023 electricity ~ +2.8 %.
2024	$ 470.00	30200	Projected	Assume −10 % cost decline, +3 % energy growth.
2025	$ 420.00	31100	Projected	NHGRI trend + IEA Electricity 2024 forecast.
2026	$ 380.00	32100	Projected	Continued learning curve; IEA +3.4 % growth.
2027	$ 340.00	33100	Projected	Moderate decline rate.
2028	$ 305.00	34100	Projected	Likely next-gen sequencer cost breakthrough.
2029	$ 275.00	34900	Projected	Electrification growth slows slightly (~2.5 %).
2030	$ 240.00	35500	Projected	Approx. −55 % cost vs 2023; +21 % energy vs 2023.

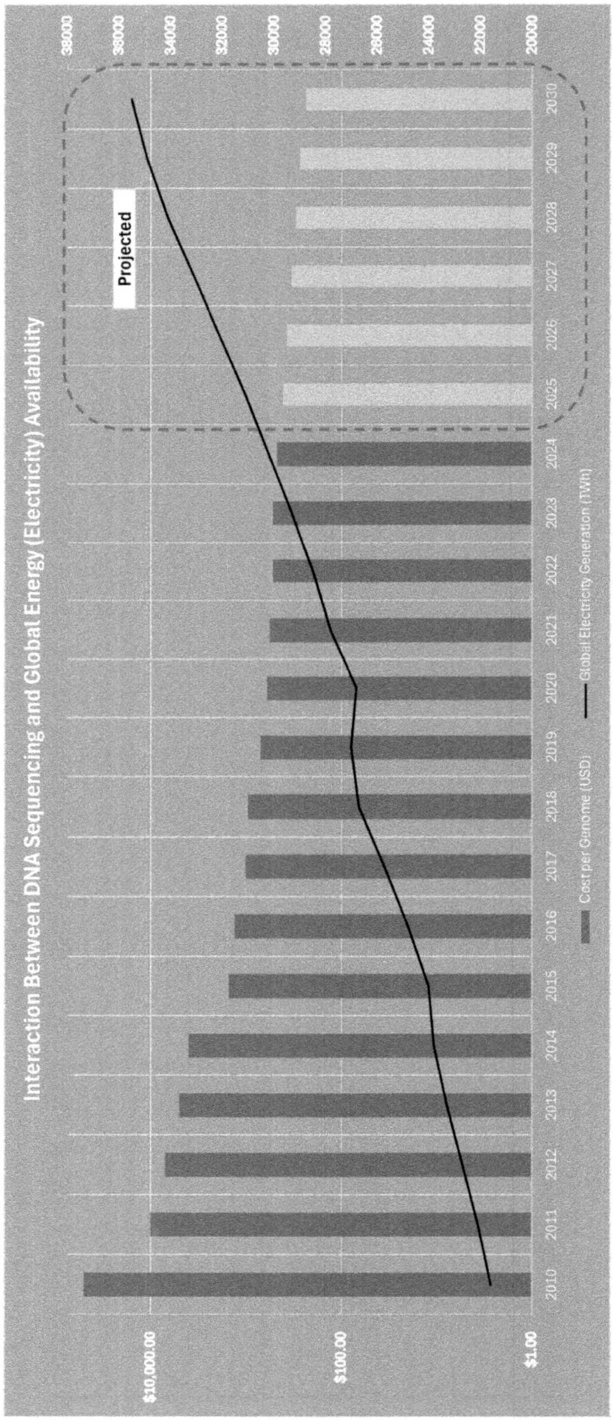
Interaction Between DNA Sequencing and Global Energy (Electricity) Availability
Projected
$10,000.00
$100.00
$1.00
20000
22000
24000
26000
28000
30000
32000
34000
36000
38000
2010
2011
2012
2013
2014
2015
2016
2017
2018
2019
2020
2021
2022
2023
2024
2025
2026
2027
2028
2029
2030
Cost per Genome (USD)
Global Electricity Generation (TWh)

Why This Should Matter to You

For healthcare providers, administrators, and patients, the relationship between **DNA sequencing and energy storage** is essential to the future of genomic medicine. As healthcare facilities increasingly rely on DNA sequencing for everything from diagnosing genetic conditions to developing personalized cancer treatments, the continuous operation of sequencing machines becomes critical. Without reliable energy storage, even minor power interruptions could delay care, compromise research, or lead to inaccurate results.

If you are a healthcare provider or administrator, investing in robust energy storage solutions ensures that your sequencing equipment remains operational at all times, safeguarding the quality and reliability of your services. This becomes especially important as more hospitals adopt precision medicine practices that rely on genomic data to guide patient care.

For patients, this technology matters because it ensures that the **genetic tests** you undergo are processed quickly and accurately, regardless of external factors like power outages or remote locations. Energy storage enables the continuity of healthcare services, allowing for more timely diagnoses and the development of personalized treatment plans that can improve outcomes.

The Future of DNA Sequencing and Energy Storage in Healthcare

As companies like **PacBio**, **Tesla**, and **Illumina** continue to innovate at the intersection of **DNA sequencing and energy storage**, healthcare will become more reliable, sustainable, and accessible. The integration of advanced energy storage systems into sequencing operations ensures that genomic data can be processed continuously, without the risk of power interruptions affecting the quality of care.

Looking ahead, this synergy will be crucial as DNA sequencing becomes more integrated into routine medical care. The ability to deliver **reliable genomic diagnostics** anywhere – whether in urban hospitals or remote clinics – will depend on the availability of stable power solutions. Energy storage ensures that the next generation of healthcare can provide personalized, data-driven treatments without being hindered by infrastructure limitations.

In short, energy storage is not just about keeping the lights on – it's about powering the future of **precision medicine** and ensuring that the breakthroughs in genomics reach every corner of the world.

10. Blockchain and Energy Storage: Securing Healthcare's Future with Sustainable Power

Blockchain technology is transforming healthcare by providing a secure, transparent, and decentralized way to manage sensitive data, such as medical records, patient information, and pharmaceutical supply chains. However, blockchain networks require substantial computational power and energy to operate efficiently. The decentralized nature of blockchain – where multiple nodes verify transactions and maintain data integrity – means that the system must run continuously, even in the event of power disruptions or grid instability.

In healthcare, where data security and reliability are paramount, power interruptions or failures could jeopardize the integrity and accessibility of critical health information. This is where **energy storage solutions** come into play. By integrating advanced energy storage systems, healthcare facilities can ensure that blockchain networks continue to function uninterrupted, even during power outages or fluctuations, safeguarding the integrity of blockchain-based health records and ensuring secure, continuous access to critical data.

Why Blockchain and Energy Storage Matter for Healthcare

Blockchain technology in healthcare is used to secure medical records, manage data sharing across institutions, and support critical applications like AI-driven diagnostics and clinical trials. For these systems to function as intended, they need continuous power to ensure the security, transparency, and immutability of the data being processed. Power disruptions not only pose a risk to the operations of blockchain networks but also threaten the availability of healthcare data during emergencies, which could be catastrophic for patient care.

Advanced energy storage solutions address this challenge by providing reliable power that keeps blockchain systems running even when the primary energy source is disrupted. This is particularly important in regions with unstable grids, as well as in hospitals and clinics where power reliability is a matter of life and death. With energy storage, healthcare facilities can ensure that blockchain networks continue to securely record and store health data, maintain real-time access to medical records, and support blockchain-based applications, regardless of external power conditions.

Leading Companies Driving Innovation at the Intersection of Blockchain and Energy Storage

1. **Power Ledger**
   - **Power Ledger**, a global leader in energy trading and blockchain solutions, is at the forefront

of integrating blockchain and energy storage. While their primary focus is on energy markets, their technology is increasingly being adopted in healthcare environments to ensure reliable, decentralized energy solutions. Power Ledger's platform allows healthcare facilities to trade excess energy generated from renewable sources, such as solar power, while maintaining a reliable energy supply for blockchain applications. By leveraging blockchain technology to optimize energy usage and integrating high-capacity batteries, Power Ledger ensures that hospitals can maintain continuous operation of blockchain networks, preserving the security and availability of critical medical records and data.

2. **LO3 Energy**
   - **LO3 Energy** is another key player utilizing blockchain and energy storage technologies to revolutionize how energy is managed and distributed. LO3's microgrid platform enables healthcare institutions to store excess energy and use blockchain to track energy consumption and distribution. This ensures that during periods of high energy demand or outages, hospitals can tap into stored energy to power their blockchain networks and keep health data secure. LO3's approach empowers healthcare providers to manage energy more efficiently while maintaining the reliability needed for blockchain-based medical record systems.
3. **Tesla Energy**
   - **Tesla Energy** is a leader in energy storage solutions with its **Powerpack** and **Megapack** systems, which provide hospitals with robust energy storage capabilities. Tesla's systems are increasingly being adopted by healthcare providers to ensure the

seamless operation of blockchain networks. By storing energy generated from renewable sources, like solar panels, Tesla's solutions provide hospitals with a backup power source that ensures the continuous operation of blockchain networks. This is particularly critical for maintaining the integrity and accessibility of blockchain-secured health records during power outages or other disruptions, ensuring that healthcare facilities can continue to operate securely and efficiently.

The Interaction between Blockchain and Energy Storage in Healthcare

Blockchain networks in healthcare need a stable power supply to maintain **data integrity, security, and availability**. Blockchain's decentralized nature – where multiple nodes work to verify and store data – requires significant computational power. Any interruption in this process could compromise the security of the system or delay access to critical healthcare data. This is especially important in hospitals and clinics that rely on blockchain for **secure medical records**, **patient information**, and **pharmaceutical supply chains**.

Energy storage solutions provide the necessary backup to ensure that blockchain networks remain operational, even in the face of power outages or unstable grids. High-capacity batteries store excess energy that can be used during periods of high demand or during grid failures, allowing blockchain systems to continue operating without interruption. In this way, energy storage and blockchain work together to enhance the resilience of healthcare data management systems, ensuring that patient information remains secure and accessible at all times.

For example, in hospitals that use blockchain to store and manage electronic health records (EHRs), an energy storage system ensures that these records remain accessible during a power outage. Without energy storage, a sudden loss of power could not only disrupt the hospital's operations but also make it difficult for healthcare providers to access patient records in critical moments. With blockchain secured by reliable energy storage, healthcare facilities can maintain a continuous flow of patient data, ensuring that the right information is always available to the right people, even in emergencies.

Energy storage also supports **sustainability** in healthcare. Many hospitals are transitioning to renewable energy sources, such as solar or wind power, to reduce their environmental impact. Blockchain is often used to manage energy consumption and distribution within these facilities, but the intermittent nature of renewable energy can be a challenge. Energy storage systems allow hospitals to store surplus renewable energy and use it when needed, ensuring that blockchain systems continue to run smoothly without relying entirely on the traditional power grid.

Why This Should Matter to You

For healthcare providers, administrators, and patients, the integration of **blockchain and energy storage** is essential for creating a **secure, reliable, and sustainable healthcare infrastructure**. Blockchain ensures the integrity and transparency of critical healthcare data, while energy storage guarantees that these systems can operate continuously, even in the event of a power outage or disruption.

As a healthcare provider, ensuring uninterrupted access to patient records, medical histories, and other critical data is vital for delivering high-quality care. With energy storage, hospitals and clinics can safeguard their blockchain-based data systems, reducing the risk of downtime and ensuring that health data is always secure and accessible. For healthcare administrators, investing in energy storage alongside blockchain offers not only improved security but also long-term cost savings through optimized energy management and a reduced reliance on the traditional grid.

For patients, this technology matters because it ensures that your healthcare data is handled securely, even in emergencies. Blockchain, backed by energy storage, provides **uninterrupted access** to your medical records and other important information, ensuring that your healthcare provider always has the data they need to make informed decisions about your care. In addition, the integration of renewable energy and energy storage systems in healthcare facilities helps create a more sustainable future for all.

The Future of Blockchain and Energy Storage in Healthcare

As companies like **Power Ledger**, **LO3 Energy**, and **Tesla Energy** continue to innovate at the intersection of **blockchain and energy storage**, the healthcare industry will become more secure, sustainable, and resilient. The combination of these technologies enables healthcare providers to maintain the security and integrity of critical health data while also optimizing energy use and reducing environmental impact.

In the future, the integration of blockchain and energy storage will become even more essential as **decentralized healthcare systems** and **AI-driven diagnostics** continue to grow. Reliable energy storage will ensure that these systems remain operational, no matter where they are deployed, making healthcare safer, more efficient, and more sustainable for everyone. By embracing these technologies, the healthcare sector can build a foundation that supports **secure, transparent, and uninterrupted care** for patients across the globe.

The Convergence of B.L.A.D.E. Technologies and Their Growing Impact on Healthcare: A Look Ahead

The convergence of AI, robotics, energy storage, DNA sequencing, and blockchain technology is creating a new frontier in healthcare. This fusion is driving the industry toward more efficient, personalized, and secure solutions, fundamentally reshaping how healthcare is delivered and experienced. The coming decade will see significant advancements across these technologies, which will revolutionize diagnostics, treatment, patient care, and the overall healthcare system. Below is a forward-looking projection of the key developments expected in the next 3, 5, and 10 years.

Over the Next 3 Years

In the near term, we can expect rapid refinement of existing technologies as they become more widely adopted across healthcare systems:

- **AI-Enhanced Diagnostics and Treatment:** AI will become integral to **diagnostic imaging**, **early detection**, and **treatment planning**. Today's capabilities in AI-assisted radiology will evolve to cover a wider range of medical conditions, with machine learning algorithms predicting patient outcomes more accurately. Companies like **Tempus**, which are using AI to analyze genomic and clinical data, will continue to improve precision medicine, enabling quicker and more accurate diagnoses for conditions like cancer and heart disease.

- **Robotic Assistance in Surgeries:** Robotics, such as the **Da Vinci Surgical System**, will see greater adoption in hospitals worldwide, particularly for **minimally invasive procedures**. These systems will become more intuitive, integrating real-time AI analysis to assist surgeons in making more precise decisions during operations, reducing recovery times for patients and minimizing complications.
- **Energy Storage Solutions:** Energy storage technology will advance, providing **uninterrupted power** to critical healthcare equipment in hospitals and **mobile health units** in remote areas. Companies like **Tesla Energy** and **NextEra** are leading the way by developing high-capacity batteries that ensure life-saving systems remain operational, even during grid failures or in areas with unstable energy access.
- **Personalized Medicine through DNA Sequencing:** DNA sequencing will continue to drive personalized medicine. Today, platforms like **Illumina** are already tailoring treatments based on patients' genetic profiles. Over the next few years, this will become more accessible, allowing for **targeted treatments** for more conditions, including rare genetic disorders, thereby improving patient outcomes.
- **Secure Data Sharing via Blockchain:** Blockchain will gain ground as a tool for **secure medical record management**, ensuring **data integrity and**

transparency. Companies like **Nebula Genomics** will refine blockchain's use in genomic data sharing, allowing for **patient-controlled data** that is securely shared among healthcare providers without compromising privacy.

Over the Next 5 Years

Five years from now, these technologies will be integrated deeply into everyday healthcare processes, leading to more transformative shifts:

- **Integrated AI Systems:** AI will be embedded in nearly every aspect of healthcare, from **patient monitoring** and **administrative workflows** to **predictive analytics** in preventive care. Systems like **Google Health** will evolve to provide **real-time health monitoring** and **automated patient care recommendations**, improving operational efficiency and overall patient outcomes.
- **Advanced Robotics in Medicine:** Robotics will advance beyond surgery into broader applications, including **rehabilitation** and **elder care**. Fully integrated AI-powered robots will assist in **physical therapy**, automating precise movements based on patient data. Companies like **Medtronic** will continue pushing the boundaries of what's possible in robotic-assisted procedures, moving toward greater autonomy and precision in the operating room.
  - **Tesla's Optimus** robot exemplifies the convergence of robotics, AI, and sustainable energy design – showcasing how energy-efficient, self-learning humanoid systems could one day assist with repetitive

care tasks, logistics, and rehabilitation in hospitals powered by renewable microgrids.

- **Sustainable Energy in Healthcare:** The widespread adoption of **advanced energy storage systems** will make healthcare facilities more resilient and sustainable. Hospitals will increasingly rely on **renewable energy**, with companies like **LO3 Energy** using blockchain to manage microgrids that optimize energy use across facilities, ensuring that critical operations remain uninterrupted.
- **Expansion of Genomic Medicine:** The role of genomic data in preventive healthcare will expand significantly. **Routine DNA sequencing** will become part of standard medical check-ups, enabling early detection of diseases like **Alzheimer's**, **diabetes**, or **heart disease** long before symptoms appear. The integration of this data into patient care systems will lead to a new era of preventive and **personalized healthcare**.
- **Blockchain Ecosystems:** Blockchain will become the **backbone of healthcare ecosystems**, enabling **seamless data exchange** across a global network of providers. This will improve patient care coordination, reduce medical errors, and enhance privacy and security through immutable data records. For example, platforms like **BurstIQ** will ensure that patient data is safely shared between hospitals, insurance companies, and research institutions.

Note: Tesla's *Optimus* humanoid robot represents a new frontier at the intersection of **robotics, AI, and sustainable energy systems**. Built on the same hardware-software ecosystem that powers Tesla's self-driving vehicles and energy storage technologies, Optimus is designed for **high energy efficiency, autonomous adaptability, and continuous**

learning through neural-network-based self-training (Tesla, 2023). In the context of healthcare, such energy-aware humanoid systems could one day perform routine physical tasks – patient lifting, mobility assistance, inventory management, or even precise rehabilitation movements – powered by renewable microgrids and advanced storage solutions. This synergy exemplifies how **AI-driven robotics, when coupled with sustainable energy infrastructure, can redefine both operational efficiency and environmental responsibility in hospitals.** (Tesla, Inc. 2023. *Tesla Optimus: Full Self-Driving AI Day Demonstration and Technical Overview*. Palo Alto, CA: Tesla AI and Energy Division.)

Over the Next 10 Years

A decade from now, the convergence of these technologies will lead to truly groundbreaking innovations and global shifts in healthcare delivery:

- **AI-Driven Innovations in Drug Discovery and Predictive Analytics:** AI will be responsible for **revolutionizing drug discovery** by identifying new drug candidates and predicting treatment outcomes based on genetic data. Companies like **Atomwise** are already using AI to sift through vast datasets and identify promising molecules for drug development. In 10 years, AI will make the process **faster**, **cheaper**, and more effective, bringing new cures to market more quickly.
- **Fully Autonomous Robots in Surgery:** Robotics will reach a point where **fully autonomous systems** perform complex surgical procedures, significantly reducing human error. These robots will integrate AI-driven insights from real-time patient data and

advanced imaging technologies, making surgeries safer, more efficient, and accessible to patients in remote locations. Companies like **Vicarious Surgical** are at the forefront of developing these capabilities. And of course, by this time, we expect autonomous humanoid robots to be ubiquitous in both repetitive tasks, but also thinking and complex structure tasks such as in a care setting (hospital or home) and actively assisting care delivery on a day-to-day basis

- **Global Energy Solutions Supporting Healthcare:** By this time, **advanced energy storage** will have solved many of the challenges related to energy access in healthcare, particularly in **developing countries**. Global health initiatives will benefit from **solar-powered hospitals** equipped with **Tesla's Powerpack systems**, providing reliable electricity to power critical healthcare technologies, even in the most remote locations.
- **Widespread DNA Sequencing and Genomic Personalization: Real-time genomic analysis** will be the norm in healthcare. DNA sequencing will not only help identify the best treatments for diseases but will also guide **preventive measures** at a population level. Companies like **PacBio** will enable healthcare providers to sequence entire populations efficiently, helping to prevent chronic diseases and tailor healthcare at the individual level.
- **Decentralized Healthcare Systems via Blockchain:** Blockchain will enable a **global decentralized healthcare system**, where patient data is securely shared across a worldwide network of healthcare providers. This system will ensure continuity of care, allowing a patient's medical history to be accessed and updated by doctors anywhere in the world, improving treatment outcomes and enhancing patient autonomy over their health data.

In Summary ...

The convergence of AI, robotics, energy storage, DNA sequencing, and blockchain is driving a seismic shift in healthcare. Over the next 3, 5, and 10 years, these technologies will not only transform how healthcare is delivered but also who can access it and how securely it is managed. This **new era of healthcare innovation** will bring about **personalized treatments**, **autonomous surgeries**, **sustainable healthcare energy solutions**, and **global data sharing networks**, ensuring that healthcare becomes more **precise**, **efficient**, and **accessible** to all.

By understanding these advancements and the trajectory they are on, healthcare professionals, administrators, researchers, scientists, and patients will be better equipped to navigate and leverage the opportunities presented by this transformative period.

THE GENESIS OF AI IN HEALTHCARE

I

Chapter 1

The Early Days of AI in Medicine

Historical Overview

Long before AI was a buzzword in Silicon Valley, it had humble beginnings in healthcare. Picture the scene: it's the 1950s, and computers are the size of rooms. The idea of using these behemoths to diagnose diseases or predict patient outcomes seems like science fiction. But that's where it all began.

In 1956, the term "artificial intelligence" was coined at a conference at Dartmouth College. It was here that visionaries started dreaming about machines that could think and learn like humans (Minsky, 1956). Fast forward to the 1970s, and we see the first AI applications in medicine. Systems like MYCIN, which was designed to diagnose bacterial infections and recommend antibiotics, were among the early pioneers. Although MYCIN never made it to clinical practice, it laid the groundwork for future developments (Shortliffe, 1976).

These early attempts at AI were like trying to bake a soufflé with a microwave. The potential was there, but

DOI: 10.4324/9781003571407-3

the tools were still a bit primitive. Yet, these efforts were crucial. They demonstrated that machines could be trained to replicate certain aspects of human thinking. Researchers like Edward Shortliffe, who developed MYCIN, and the creators of INTERNIST-I, William B. Schwartz and Randolph A. Miller, became the trailblazers in this new frontier. Their work showed that, with enough data and the right algorithms, AI could indeed make meaningful contributions to medicine (Schwartz & Miller, 1980).

The MYCIN System: A Pioneer in Medical AI

One of the earliest and most notable AI systems was MYCIN, developed in the early 1970s at Stanford University. MYCIN was designed to diagnose bacterial infections and recommend antibiotics. It was a rule-based expert system, meaning that it used a series of if-then statements to mimic the decision-making process of a human expert (Shortliffe, 1976).

MYCIN's development was groundbreaking. It was one of the first systems to demonstrate that a computer could, in some ways, think like a doctor. Despite its potential, MYCIN never made it to clinical practice due to various limitations, including computational power and regulatory hurdles. However, it laid the groundwork for future developments in medical AI.

INTERNIST-I: Tackling Complex Diagnoses

Around the same time, another pioneering AI system, INTERNIST-I, was developed by researchers at the University of Pittsburgh. INTERNIST-I aimed to assist with the diagnosis of complex diseases, particularly in internal medicine (Miller et al., 1982). It worked by matching patient symptoms with a vast database of medical knowledge to suggest possible diagnoses.

While INTERNIST-I had its limitations, such as a lack of flexibility and the inability to handle incomplete data, it represented a significant step forward. It showed that AI could be a valuable tool in diagnosing complex medical conditions, paving the way for more advanced systems.

The Role of Early Researchers and Institutions

The progress in AI healthcare wouldn't have been possible without the contributions of numerous visionaries and institutions. Apart from Edward Shortliffe and Geoffrey Hinton, other key figures include Fei-Fei Li, whose work in computer vision has been instrumental, and Andrew Ng, a pioneer in machine learning and co-founder of Google Brain.

Institutions like MIT, Stanford, and Google DeepMind have been at the forefront of AI research. Google's DeepMind, for instance, developed AlphaGo, an AI that defeated the world champion Go player, demonstrating the power of deep learning and reinforcement learning. DeepMind's subsequent work in healthcare, particularly in predicting patient deterioration and diagnosing eye diseases, has set new standards for what AI can achieve (Silver et al., 2016).

Challenges Faced by Early AI Systems

The early AI systems faced significant challenges, primarily due to the limitations of the technology at the time. Computers in the 1970s were slow and lacked the computational power needed to run complex algorithms. Data storage was also limited, making it difficult to manage the vast amounts of information required for AI systems.

Furthermore, these early systems were rule-based, meaning that they relied on a predefined set of rules to make decisions. This made them rigid and unable to handle the variability and complexity of real-world medical cases. Despite these limitations, the early researchers persisted, driven by the belief that AI could transform healthcare.

The Impact of Early AI Systems

Although MYCIN and INTERNIST-I never made it to clinical practice, their impact on the field of medical AI cannot be overstated. They demonstrated that AI could be a valuable tool in healthcare, inspiring future generations of researchers to continue the work.

These early systems also laid the foundation for the development of more advanced AI technologies. The lessons learned from MYCIN and INTERNIST-I helped researchers understand the limitations of rule-based systems and paved the way for the development of machine learning and neural networks, which have since revolutionized the field.

Takeaways

The early days of AI in healthcare were marked by groundbreaking innovations and significant challenges. Researchers like Edward Shortliffe and institutions like Stanford and MIT played a crucial role in laying the groundwork for the development of AI systems that have the potential to transform healthcare.

As we move forward, it's important to remember the lessons learned from these early pioneers. The limitations and challenges they faced have helped shape the development of more advanced AI systems, paving the way for a future where AI can truly revolutionize healthcare.

Bibliography

Miller, R. A., Pople, H. E., & Myers, J. D. (1982). "INTERNIST-I, an experimental computer-based diagnostic consultant for general internal medicine." New England Journal of Medicine, 307(8), 468–476.

Minsky, M. (1956). "Steps toward artificial intelligence." Proceedings of the IRE, 49(1), 8–30.

Schwartz, W. B., & Miller, R. A. (1980). "The use of the Internist-I computer program as a consultant for general internal medicine." Computers and Biomedical Research, 13(5), 452–470.

Shortliffe, E. H. (1976). "Computer-Based Medical Consultations: MYCIN." Elsevier.

Silver, D. et al. (2016). "Mastering the game of Go with deep neural networks and tree search." Nature, 529(7587), 484–489.

Chapter 2

AI Milestones in Healthcare

Key Developments and Breakthroughs

The journey from those early days to the present has been marked by significant milestones. The evolution of artificial intelligence (AI) in healthcare is a fascinating story of innovation, perseverance, and sometimes pure serendipity. As we navigate through these milestones, let's also glance at what was happening in the broader world, because, let's face it, history isn't made in a vacuum.

The 1980s: The Dawn of Personal Computing and AI in Healthcare

In the 1980s, the world was introduced to personal computers. IBM launched its first PC in 1981, and suddenly, computing power was within reach of not just universities and businesses but also homes. This decade also saw the rise of Microsoft and Apple, as well as the birth of iconic video games like Pac-Man and Super Mario Bros.

DOI: 10.4324/9781003571407-4

In healthcare, the 1980s marked a significant leap forward for AI. The field saw the development of the first expert systems. An example is INTERNIST-I, which evolved into the Quick Medical Reference (QMR). QMR aimed to assist physicians in diagnosing complex diseases. It was a rule-based system that required users to input symptoms and lab results, which the system would then analyze to provide possible diagnoses (Miller et al., 1986).

The 1990s: The Internet Boom and AI's Growing Role

The 1990s were a transformative time. The internet boom reshaped how we communicated, worked, and entertained ourselves. Remember the sound of dial-up internet? Iconic. This decade also saw the release of the first-ever website in 1991, and by the mid-1990s, the World Wide Web had become a household term. Movies like "Jurassic Park" and "The Matrix" captivated audiences with their futuristic themes, hinting at the burgeoning interest in technology's possibilities.

In the realm of healthcare, AI made strides with natural language processing (NLP). IBM's Watson wasn't around yet, but the foundations were being laid. Researchers developed early NLP systems to assist in medical record-keeping and information retrieval. These systems aimed to reduce the paperwork burden on healthcare professionals, allowing them to focus more on patient care (Friedman et al., 1994).

The 2000s: The Rise of Social Media and AI in Imaging

Ah, the 2000s. The decade of social media's inception, with platforms like Facebook (2004) and Twitter (2006) changing how we connected and communicated. It was also the era of the iPhone (2007), which revolutionized the smartphone industry and our daily lives. And who can forget the cultural phenomenon of reality TV shows like "American Idol" and "Survivor"?

In healthcare, the 2000s were transformative for AI, especially in medical imaging. The integration of AI in radiology began to gain traction. Systems like Computer-Aided Detection (CAD) were developed to assist radiologists in identifying abnormalities in medical images, such as mammograms, CT scans, and MRIs. These tools aimed to improve accuracy and reduce diagnostic errors, helping detect conditions like cancer at earlier, more treatable stages (Doi, 2007).

The 2010s: The Age of Big Data, AI, and Pop Culture Explosion

The 2010s were dominated by big data, the explosion of mobile technology, and the mainstreaming of AI. It was a decade where phrases like "there's an app for that" became part of our everyday lexicon. Pop culture saw the rise of streaming services like Netflix and binge-watching TV shows. "Game of Thrones" and "Breaking Bad" became cultural touchstones, and social media continued to dominate our lives, with Instagram and Snapchat becoming hugely popular.

In healthcare, the 2010s witnessed the true coming-of-age for AI. IBM Watson made headlines in 2011 by defeating human champions on "Jeopardy!", showcasing AI's potential to process and analyze vast amounts of data rapidly and accurately (Ferrucci et al., 2010). This was a watershed moment, leading to Watson's application in oncology, where it helped oncologists develop personalized treatment plans by analyzing medical literature, clinical trial data, and patient records.

Deep learning, a subset of machine learning, also emerged as a powerhouse. In 2012, a deep learning algorithm developed by Geoffrey Hinton and his team achieved a breakthrough in image recognition, reducing the error rate in the ImageNet competition by half (Krizhevsky et al., 2012). This had profound implications for medical imaging, leading to AI systems capable of analyzing X-rays, MRIs, and CT scans with remarkable precision.

The Late 2010s and Early 2020s: AI during the Pandemic

The end of the 2010s and the early 2020s were marked by significant global events, most notably the COVID-19 pandemic. This period also saw a surge in AI applications across various sectors. In pop culture, streaming services became even more dominant as people stayed home, and shows like "Tiger King" became unexpected hits.

In healthcare, the pandemic underscored the vital role of AI. AI-powered platforms like BlueDot were among the first to detect the outbreak of COVID-19 by analyzing vast amounts of data, including news reports and airline ticketing data, to predict the spread of infectious diseases (Miller, 2020). AI also accelerated vaccine development. Moderna used AI to optimize mRNA sequences for its COVID-19 vaccine, significantly speeding up the research and development process (Moderna, 2020).

Influential Figures and Institutions

The progress in AI healthcare wouldn't have been possible without the contributions of numerous visionaries and institutions. Apart from Edward Shortliffe and Geoffrey Hinton, other key figures include Fei-Fei Li, whose work in computer vision has been instrumental, and Andrew Ng, a pioneer in machine learning and co-founder of Google Brain.

Institutions like MIT, Stanford, and Google DeepMind have been at the forefront of AI research. Google's DeepMind, for instance, developed AlphaGo, an AI that defeated the world champion Go player, demonstrating the power of deep learning and reinforcement learning. DeepMind's subsequent work in healthcare, particularly in predicting patient deterioration and diagnosing eye diseases, has set new standards for what AI can achieve (Silver et al., 2016).

AI Milestones: A Timeline

1950s–1970s: Foundations and Early Developments

- **1956:** The term "artificial intelligence" is coined at the Dartmouth Conference.
- **1970s:** Development of MYCIN and INTERNIST-I, early AI systems for medical diagnosis.

1980s: The Rise of Expert Systems

- **1980s:** Introduction of personal computers; development of Quick Medical Reference (QMR) as an evolution of INTERNIST-I (Miller et al., 1986).

1990s: Natural Language Processing

- **1990s:** The internet boom; early NLP systems for medical record-keeping and information retrieval (Friedman et al., 1994).

2000s: AI in Medical Imaging

- **2000s:** Development of Computer-Aided Detection (CAD) systems for radiology (Doi, 2007).

2010s: Big Data and Deep Learning

- **2011:** IBM Watson wins "Jeopardy!" (Ferrucci et al., 2010).

- **2012:** Breakthrough in deep learning by Geoffrey Hinton's team (Krizhevsky et al., 2012).
- **2013:** IBM Watson applied in oncology for personalized treatment plans.

Late 2010s–2020s: AI and the Pandemic

- **2020:** AI detects COVID-19 outbreak (Miller, 2020).
- **2020:** Moderna uses AI for COVID-19 vaccine development (Moderna, 2020).
- **2023:** Over 220 AI/ML-enabled medical devices cleared by the U.S. Food and Drug Administration (FDA), signaling a rapid growth phase.
- **2024:** The FDA issues draft guidance on "Artificial Intelligence-Enabled Device Software Functions" for lifecycle management of AI/ML medical devices.
- **2025:**
  - The FDA publishes a Request for Public Comment on measuring and evaluating AI-enabled medical device performance in real-world settings (Docket FDA-2025-N-4203) (U.S. Food and Drug Administration, 2025).
  - Canada's "2025 Watch List" identifies top emerging AI technologies in healthcare (e.g., AI for notetaking, disease detection, and remote monitoring) and key issues such as bias, data governance, and accountability (https://pubmed.ncbi.nlm.nih.gov/40294189/).
  - A news-reported case: Aidoc Rib Fracture Triage AI receives FDA clearance for rib-fracture triage, February 2025.

Looking Ahead....

Looking Ahead: 2026–2027

AI in healthcare is moving from experimentation to large-scale, regulated deployment. The next two years will mark a transition from isolated pilots to embedded, intelligent systems that span diagnostics, clinical workflows, operations, and public health. As AI matures, it will increasingly serve as both a **clinical partner** and a **digital infrastructure layer** underpinning the future of care delivery.

1. ***Scale-Up of AI in Care Delivery***
   By 2026, AI adoption will shift from early pilot programs to widespread operational integration across hospitals and clinics. Health systems will rely on AI to automate clinical documentation, streamline patient triage, and support chronic disease management. Smaller and community-based providers will leverage cloud-based AI services to extend care capacity and improve access. This scale-up will be driven by improvements in data interoperability, cloud architecture, and pre-trained healthcare-specific models.
2. ***Multimodal and Agentic AI for Clinical Decision-Making***
   By 2027, "multimodal" AI models – those combining imaging, genomics, lab data, and patient narratives – will begin influencing complex decision-making in oncology, cardiology, and neurology. These models will integrate structured and unstructured data to deliver more holistic patient insights.
   Simultaneously, "agentic AI" systems – semi-autonomous agents embedded within electronic health record (EHR) workflows – will begin managing low-risk, repetitive decisions, freeing clinicians to focus on empathy, judgment, and higher-complexity cases.
3. ***Generative AI and Documentation Automation***
   Generative AI will play a central role in reducing administrative burden. By late 2026, the majority of leading U.S. health systems are expected to deploy AI-based clinical documentation assistants to draft notes,

discharge summaries, and patient communications. McKinsey & Company (2024) by some estimates, this could return 15–20% of physician time back to patient care. Integrated large language models (LLMs) will also improve patient education materials, enhancing understanding and adherence.

4. ***Real-World Evidence and Regulatory Alignment***

   The regulatory landscape will mature significantly. The European Union's **AI Act** (effective August 2026) will establish harmonized standards for transparency, bias mitigation, and accountability in AI-driven health systems. In the United States, the FDA's ongoing initiatives for adaptive algorithm monitoring will align clinical AI systems with real-world evidence frameworks. Hospitals will embed AI performance dashboards into quality governance structures to continuously track safety, bias, and accuracy.

5. ***Market Growth and Infrastructure Evolution***

   According to Grand View Research (2025), the global AI healthcare market – valued at **$26.6 billion in 2024** – is projected to grow at a **38.6% CAGR**, reaching **$187.7 billion by 2030**. Much of this growth will come from infrastructure investments in data platforms, edge computing, and interoperability layers that enable enterprise-wide deployment rather than isolated pilots.

6. ***Equity, Access, and Global Deployment***

   AI will increasingly extend care to underserved and remote regions. Advances in federated learning and privacy-preserving analytics will enable models to train on decentralized data without exposing sensitive information. This will help address global inequities in access to quality care and support the World Health Organization's ongoing agenda for ethical and equitable digital health (WHO, 2021).

7. ***Integration with Other Emerging Technologies***
By 2027, AI will operate in concert with robotics, genomics, and digital twins to create *systems of systems* – self-learning, continuously improving ecosystems that bridge clinical, operational, and population health domains. Predictive and generative AI will power robotic assistants, wearables, and hospital energy systems alike, completing the convergence between intelligence, automation, and sustainability.

Conclusion

AI's journey in healthcare has been a rollercoaster of innovation, setbacks, and breakthroughs. From the early days of MYCIN (Shortliffe, 1976) and INTERNIST-I (Miller et al., 1982) to the advanced deep learning algorithms of today, AI has come a long way. Each milestone, set against the backdrop of broader societal changes, highlights AI's transformative potential.

As we look into the future, it's clear that AI will continue to revolutionize healthcare. The challenge for healthcare providers, payers, pharmacies, drug manufacturers, and DME providers is to stay ahead of the curve, leveraging AI to improve patient outcomes, streamline operations, and drive innovation.

Bibliography

Doi, K. (2007). "Computer-aided diagnosis in medical imaging: Historical review, current status and future potential." Computerized Medical Imaging and Graphics, 31(4–5), 198–211. https://doi.org/10.1016/j.compmedimag.2007.02.002

European Parliament and Council of the European Union. (2024). "Regulation (EU) 2024/1689 laying down harmonised rules on artificial intelligence (Artificial Intelligence Act)." Official Journal of the European Union. Retrieved from https://eur-lex.europa.eu/eli/reg/2024/1689/oj

Ferrucci, D., et al. (2010). "Building Watson: An overview of the DeepQA Project." AI Magazine, 31(3), 59–79.

Friedman, C., et al. (1994). "A general natural-language text processor for clinical radiology." Journal of the American Medical Informatics Association, 1(2), 161–174.

Grand View Research (2025) https://www.grandviewresearch.com/industry-analysis/artificial-intelligence-ai-healthcare-market

Krizhevsky, A., Sutskever, I., & Hinton, G. E. (2012). "Imagenet classification with deep convolutional neural networks." Advances in Neural Information Processing Systems, 25, 1097–1105.

McKinsey & Company. (2024). "Generative AI in healthcare: Current trends and future outlook." Retrieved from https://www.mckinsey.com/industries/healthcare/our-insights/generative-ai-in-healthcare-current-trends-and-future-outlook

Miller, J. (2020). "Artificial intelligence and COVID-19: Can AI help in the fight against the coronavirus?" Forbes. Retrieved from https://www.forbes.com

Miller, R. A., Masarie, F. E., & Myers, J. D. (1986). "Quick Medical Reference (QMR) for diagnostic assistance." M.D. Computing, 3(5), 34–48.

Miller, R. A., Pople, H. E., &, & Myers, J. D.(1982). "INTERNIST-II, an experimental computer-based diagnostic consultant for general internal medicine." New England Journal of Medicine, 307(8), 468–476.

Moderna. (2020). "Moderna's work on the COVID-19 vaccine." Retrieved from https://www.modernatx.com

Shortliffe, E. H. (1976). "Computer-Based Medical Consultations: MYCIN." Elsevier.

Silver, D., et al. (2016). "Mastering the game of Go with deep neural networks and tree search." Nature, 529(7587), 484–489.

U.S. Food and Drug Administration. (2025). "Artificial Intelligence and Machine Learning (AI/ML)-enabled medical devices." Retrieved from https://www.fda.gov/medical-devices/software-medical-device-samd/artificial-intelligence-and-machine-learning-aiml-enabled-medical-devices

World Health Organization. (2021). "Ethics and governance of artificial intelligence for health: WHO guidance." Retrieved from https://www.who.int/publications/i/item/9789240029200

THE PRESENT LANDSCAPE

II

Chapter 3

AI in Healthcare Providers

Enhancing Diagnostics and Treatment

The integration of Artificial Intelligence (AI) into healthcare providers' arsenals is like upgrading from a bicycle to a high-speed train. The potential for improved diagnostics, personalized treatment plans, and streamlined operations is vast. However, as with any powerful tool, success hinges on how well it's integrated into currently accepted workflows, technology systems, processes and quite frankly, institutional, organizational, and personal systems of value and belief. Let's look at a few case studies and examples of where and how this promise of AI in healthcare providers is coming to be true and real.

The Promise of AI in Healthcare

Imagine a world where diagnosing diseases isn't a guessing game but a precise science. AI promises to make this world a reality. By analyzing vast amounts of medical data, AI can identify patterns

DOI: 10.4324/9781003571407-6

and provide insights that even the most experienced physicians might miss. For instance, AI algorithms can analyze medical images faster and often more accurately than human radiologists. A study published in *Nature* in 2020 revealed that Google's AI system could detect breast cancer in mammograms with greater accuracy than radiologists (McKinney et al., 2020).

In oncology, AI is making strides by personalizing cancer treatment. Beyond just reading data, AI helps streamline and optimize care pathways. A notable example is Memorial Sloan Kettering Cancer Center, which has developed its own AI models to assist oncologists in creating individualized treatment plans, ensuring that patients receive the most current, data-driven care available.

Case Studies: When AI Efforts Succeeded…

Here, we highlight five case studies where healthcare providers have successfully integrated AI, improving care for patients in meaningful ways.

Massachusetts General Hospital: AI for Imaging and Predictive Analytics

Massachusetts General Hospital (MGH) has long been at the forefront of AI in healthcare. The hospital's Center for Clinical Data Science developed AI algorithms for diagnosing conditions such as pneumonia, sepsis, and lung cancer by analyzing chest X-rays and other medical images. MGH also uses AI to predict patient readmissions, optimizing both care and resource allocation.

Why It Worked:

1. **Collaboration with Clinicians:** Clinicians were deeply involved in the AI development process, ensuring that the tools were practical and met real clinical needs.

2. **High-Quality Data:** MGH invested in high-quality, annotated medical data, crucial for training accurate AI models.
3. **Iterative Testing and Implementation:** The hospital continuously tested and refined AI tools, integrating feedback from both medical staff and patients.

Near-Real-Life Example: A patient presents at site of care with symptoms of pneumonia. The AI-assisted radiology tool flags a subtle anomaly on the patient's X-ray that was missed in the initial assessment. This leads to early intervention, and the patient's condition improves rapidly, avoiding what could have been a life-threatening complication. In the back end, both the manual X-ray review processes and personnel are given this feedback to help them detect even better next instance; algorithms identification is marked as a "true positive," thereby reinforcing its learning and identification for future cases

Key Takeaway: Successful AI integration requires reliable technology, strong clinician partnerships, access to high-quality data, and ongoing refinement of the technology and its use.

Kaiser Permanente: Improving Chronic Disease Management

Kaiser Permanente, one of the largest healthcare systems in the United States, uses AI to manage chronic diseases like diabetes and hypertension. The organization developed an AI-driven system that analyzes patient data to predict which patients are at a higher risk of disease progression or hospitalization. These insights allow care teams to intervene early, preventing complications and improving overall health outcomes.

Why It Worked:

1. **Population Health Focus:** AI was designed with the goal of managing large populations and detecting potential health risks early.
2. **Comprehensive Data Integration:** Kaiser Permanente utilized its vast electronic health record (EHR) system, ensuring that the AI had access to a wide range of patient data.
3. **Scalability:** The AI system was designed to be scalable, providing insights across Kaiser Permanente's vast network of hospitals and clinics.

Near-Real-Life Example: A patient with diabetes is identified by the AI rising-risk system as being at risk of developing severe kidney complications. Thanks to this early detection, the patient is enrolled in a specialized care program that includes dietary changes, medication adjustments, and regular monitoring. As a result, the patient's kidney function improves, preventing the need for more invasive treatments.

Key Takeaway: AI can be a powerful tool for managing chronic diseases when it leverages extensive patient data and targets early interventions. Early interventions avoid the need for complex, undesirable, costly, and preventable care. As with the example before, this true-positive identification is served to the AI system through a feedback loop, thereby allowing it to strengthen its early identification pathways for future applications

Cleveland Clinic: AI for Cardiology

The Cleveland Clinic has been a leader in using AI to enhance cardiovascular care. The clinic developed an AI-powered tool that can predict heart disease and stroke by analyzing patterns in patients' EHR data. The AI identifies patients at risk and provides clinicians with recommendations for personalized treatment plans, reducing the likelihood of cardiac events.

Why It Worked:

1. **Data-Driven Personalization:** The AI tool provided personalized insights based on each patient's unique health profile, ensuring that treatments were tailored to individual needs.
2. **Proactive Care:** The AI was not reactive but proactive, identifying potential issues before they developed into serious conditions.
3. **Cross-Departmental Collaboration:** The Cleveland Clinic involved not just cardiologists but also data scientists and IT professionals, ensuring a comprehensive approach to AI integration.

Near-Real-Life Example: A middle-aged patient with no significant history of heart disease is flagged by the cardiovascular care AI system as being at high risk for a future cardiac event. Upon further examination, the patient is found to have early signs of coronary artery disease. Thanks to the AI tool, the patient receives timely interventions, including lifestyle changes and medication, significantly reducing their risk of heart attack.

Key Takeaway: AI can play a crucial role in preventive care, identifying risks early and enabling clinicians to act before a condition becomes life-threatening. In future, as more and more of this identification technology gets transferred to be even closer and therefore more real time – e.g. the patient's wearable devices (like a watch) or other DME that they use on a daily of regular basis – the timeliness of such identification will only improve.

Mount Sinai Health System: AI for Predicting Sepsis

Mount Sinai Health System in New York developed an AI tool that predicts the onset of sepsis, a life-threatening condition caused by infection. The AI analyzes patient data in real time, looking for subtle changes in vital signs and lab results that could indicate the early stages of sepsis. This allows clinicians to intervene earlier, improving patient survival rates.

Why It Worked:

1. **Real-Time Data Analysis:** The AI system worked in real time, providing clinicians with up-to-the-minute insights.
2. **Seamless Integration into Workflow:** The AI tool was embedded into the existing clinical workflow, ensuring that doctors and nurses could use it without disrupting their normal routines.
3. **Clear Clinical Value:** The focus on sepsis, a condition that requires rapid response, ensured the AI tool provided clear value by saving lives.

Near-Real-Life Example: A patient in the ICU begins showing subtle signs of distress that weren't immediately noticeable to the human eye. However, the AI tool flags the patient as at risk for sepsis. Thanks to the early warning, the care team initiates treatment immediately, preventing the condition from worsening and saving the patient's life.

Key Takeaway: AI's ability to analyze real-time data can significantly improve patient outcomes by allowing clinicians to respond to life-threatening conditions earlier.

Mayo Clinic: AI for Personalized Cancer Treatment

Mayo Clinic has long been a leader in cancer research and treatment, and its use of AI has further elevated its ability to provide personalized care. Mayo Clinic collaborated with Tempus, an AI-driven company, to develop models that analyze patient genomic data to identify the most effective cancer treatments based on the patient's unique genetic makeup.

Why It Worked:

1. **Cutting-Edge Genomic Data:** Mayo Clinic's access to extensive genomic data allowed the AI to recommend highly personalized treatment plans.
2. **Collaboration with AI Experts:** By partnering with Tempus, Mayo Clinic leveraged external expertise to develop advanced AI tools tailored for oncology.
3. **Focus on Personalization:** The primary aim of the AI was to tailor treatment plans specifically to each patient's genetic profile, making the treatment more effective and reducing side effects.

Real-Life Example: A patient with a rare form of cancer undergoes treatment at Mayo Clinic. The AI analyzes the patient's genomic data and recommended a targeted therapy that had not been considered in the initial treatment plan. The new therapy significantly improves the patient's response to treatment, leading to better outcomes and an improved quality of life.

Key Takeaway: AI's ability to analyze complex genomic data can lead to highly personalized and effective cancer treatments, improving patient outcomes.

Case Studies: When AI Efforts Failed…

Not every effort in this area has been successful, however; in fact, the road to successes is littered with many failures. Let's review a couple of examples to understand the details.

IBM Watson for Oncology at MD Anderson Cancer Center

IBM's Watson for Oncology was initially touted as a revolutionary AI system to assist doctors in diagnosing and treating cancer. MD Anderson Cancer Center aimed to integrate Watson into their oncology care to provide recommendations based on the vast amounts of clinical data and medical literature. However, the project was discontinued after several years due to high costs and integration challenges.

Why It Failed:

- **Data Complexity:** Watson struggled to understand the complexity of clinical data, which included both structured and unstructured data from patient records. The data wasn't always clean or standardized, leading to inaccurate recommendations.
- **Overpromised Results:** Watson's capabilities were overestimated. It could not deliver on the promise of offering personalized cancer treatment recommendations based on real-time data.
- **Lack of Clinician Buy-In:** Clinicians found the AI system difficult to integrate into their existing workflows, and many were skeptical of its value. As a result, it wasn't fully adopted, and its use was limited.

What Needed to Be True:

- AI tools need to manage both structured and unstructured data more effectively.
- Successful integration requires strong clinician engagement from the beginning to ensure the AI system fits into the clinical workflow.
- A realistic understanding of AI capabilities is essential – Watson overpromised and underdelivered, creating frustration among users.

AI Diagnostic Tools in Schizophrenia Trials

In a real-world trial involving AI tools to assess schizophrenia patients, the AI systems, which were initially trained on highly specific clinical trial data, failed when applied to broader patient populations. The systems performed well in controlled environments but faltered when exposed to the variability of real-world patient data.

Why It Failed:

- **Generalizability Issues:** The AI was trained on a limited and controlled dataset, meaning it lacked the diversity to handle the broad range of schizophrenia cases in real clinical settings.
- **Bias in Data:** The training data was biased, not accounting for diverse patient demographics, which led to the AI system misdiagnosing or missing key symptoms in patients outside the training group.
- **Clinical Mistrust:** Similar to other AI failures, clinicians were reluctant to rely on an AI tool that produced inconsistent results, limiting its adoption.

What Needed to Be True:

- AI systems need to be trained on diverse, real-world data to ensure they can handle the variability found in actual clinical settings.
- Clearer communication with clinicians about the system's limitations and providing better training could improve trust and adoption.
- AI tools should be continually tested and refined with real-world patient data before full deployment (Price, 2019).

These examples demonstrate the importance of data quality, clinician buy-in, and realistic expectations for AI technology in healthcare. Addressing these factors can help avoid costly failures and improve the chances of successful integration.

Our Learnings – The "Why" Behind Successes and Failures

Success Factors

- **Clear Objectives:** Successful AI projects start with clear, measurable objectives. Knowing what you want to achieve helps in selecting the right technology and setting realistic expectations.
- **Stakeholder Buy-In:** Getting buy-in from all stakeholders, including clinicians, IT staff, and executives, is crucial. When everyone is on board, the transition is smoother, and adoption rates are higher.
- **Data Management:** High-quality, well-annotated data is the backbone of any AI system. Without it, even the most sophisticated algorithms will fail.
- **Continuous Learning:** AI systems need constant updates and refinements. Organizations that treat AI as a one-time project often see their systems become outdated and less effective over time.

Failure Factors

- **Lack of Clear Strategy:** Jumping on the AI bandwagon without a clear strategy is a recipe for disaster. Without defined goals, projects can quickly lose direction and fail to deliver value.
- **Poor Data Quality:** Garbage in, garbage out. If the data used to train AI models is poor, the results will be unreliable. Ensuring data quality is non-negotiable.
- **Resistance to Change:** AI implementation often fails when there is significant resistance from staff. This can be due to a lack of understanding, fear of job loss, or simply being set in old ways.
- **Overreliance on Vendors:** While vendors can provide valuable technology, overreliance without internal expertise can lead to challenges in customization, integration, and troubleshooting.

Practical Do's and Don'ts for AI Success at Healthcare Providers

Do's

- **Do Involve Clinicians Early and Often:** Ensure that the end-users of AI systems, like doctors and nurses, are involved in the development and implementation process. Their insights are invaluable.
- **Do Invest in Data Quality:** High-quality data is essential for accurate AI models. Invest in proper data collection, cleaning, and annotation processes.
- **Do Start Small and Scale:** Begin with pilot projects to test AI systems on a small scale. Learn from these pilots before scaling up to full deployment.
- **Do Provide Comprehensive Training:** Ensure that all users are adequately trained on how to use AI tools. This includes not only technical training but also understanding the benefits and limitations of AI.
- **Do Monitor and Refine Continuously:** AI systems require ongoing monitoring and refinement. Establish processes for regular updates and performance assessments.

Don'ts

- **Don't Ignore the Human Element:** AI is a tool to augment human capabilities, not replace them. Ensure that the human element remains central to care delivery.
- **Don't Skimp on Security:** AI systems often handle sensitive patient data. Prioritize robust security measures to protect this information.
- **Don't Rely Solely on Vendors:** While vendors provide valuable technology, develop internal expertise to customize and troubleshoot AI systems effectively.
- **Don't Overpromise:** Set realistic expectations for what AI can achieve. Avoid hyping capabilities that aren't yet feasible.

- **Don't Neglect Ethical Considerations:** Address ethical issues such as bias and fairness proactively. Ensure that AI systems are transparent and accountable.

Conclusion

The integration of AI in healthcare providers is not just a technological upgrade; it's a transformative journey. By learning from past successes and failures, and by following practical guidelines, healthcare providers can harness the power of AI to improve patient care, streamline operations, and drive innovation. The future is bright, and with the right approach, AI can be a catalyst for remarkable advancements in healthcare.

Bibliography

Doi, K. (2007). "Computer-aided diagnosis in medical imaging: Historical review, current status and future potential." Computerized Medical Imaging and Graphics, 31(4–5), 198–211. https://doi.org/10.1016/j.compmedimag.2007.02.002

Ferrucci, D., Brown, E., Chu-Carroll, J., Fan, J., Gondek, D., Kalyanpur, A. A., Lally, A., Murdock, J. W., Nyberg, E., Prager, J., Schlaefer, N., & Welty, C. (2010). "Building Watson: An overview of the DeepQA project." AI Magazine, 31(3), 59–79. https://doi.org/10.1609/aimag.v31i3.2303

Krizhevsky, A., Sutskever, I., & Hinton, G. E. (2012). "ImageNet classification with deep convolutional neural networks." Advances in Neural Information Processing Systems, 25, 1097–1105. https://papers.nips.cc/paper/4824-imagenet-classification-with-deep-convolutional-neural-networks

McKinney, S. M., Sieniek, M., Godbole, V., Godwin, J., Antropova, N., Ashrafian, H., Back, T., Chesus, M., Corrado, G. S., Darzi, A., Etemadi, M., Garcia-Vicente, F., Gilbert, F. J., Halling-Brown, M., Hassabis, D., Jansen, S., Karthikesalingam, A.,

Kelly, C. J., King, D., … Shetty, S. (2020). "International evaluation of an AI system for breast cancer screening." Nature, 577(7788), 89–94. https://doi.org/10.1038/s41586-019-1799-6

Memorial Sloan Kettering Cancer Center. (2012, March 22). "Memorial Sloan-Kettering Cancer Center, IBM to collaborate in applying Watson technology to help oncologists [Press release]." https://www.mskcc.org/news-releases/mskcc-ibm-collaborate-applying-watson-technology-help-oncologists

Moderna, Inc. (2020). "Moderna's work on a potential vaccine against COVID-19." https://www.modernatx.com/modernas-work-potential-vaccine-against-covid-19

Price, W. N. (2019, October 30). "Who's at fault when AI fails in health care?" Stanford HAI. https://hai.stanford.edu/news/whos-fault-when-ai-fails-health-care

Ross, C., & Swetlitz, I. (2017, September 5). "IBM pitched its Watson supercomputer as a revolution in cancer care. It's nowhere close." STAT News. https://www.statnews.com/2017/09/05/watson-ibm-cancer/

Silver, D., Huang, A., Maddison, C. J., Guez, A., Sifre, L., van den Driessche, G., Schrittwieser, J., Antonoglou, I., Panneershelvam, V., Lanctot, M., Dieleman, S., Grewe, D., Nham, J., Kalchbrenner, N., Sutskever, I., Lillicrap, T., Leach, M., Kavukcuoglu, K., Graepel, T., & Hassabis, D. (2016). "Mastering the game of Go with deep neural networks and tree search." Nature, 529(7587), 484–489. https://doi.org/10.1038/nature16961

Chapter 4

Machine Learning and Generative AI in Payer Operations

Artificial Intelligence (AI) is revolutionizing the operations of healthcare payers – insurance companies – by streamlining processes, improving patient outcomes, and reducing costs. From call center optimization to care management, disease management, and fraud detection and prevention, Machine Learning (ML) and Generative AI are driving these transformations. In this chapter, we will explore detailed use cases across the value chain for payers and conclude with practical do's and don'ts.

Call Center Optimization

Call centers are the nerve centers of payer operations, handling inquiries about claims, coverage, and benefits. AI-driven solutions are making these operations more efficient and customer-centric.

DOI: 10.4324/9781003571407-7

Use Case: Natural Language Processing for Enhanced Customer Service

Natural Language Processing (NLP) enables AI to understand and respond to customer queries in real time, enhancing the efficiency and effectiveness of call centers.

Example: Anthem Inc. Anthem implemented an AI-powered virtual assistant to handle routine customer service queries. This assistant uses NLP to understand and respond to questions about benefits, claims, and coverage, handling thousands of interactions simultaneously.

Why It Works:

- **Efficiency:** Reduces wait times and handles high volumes of inquiries.
- **Consistency:** Provides accurate and consistent information.
- **Scalability:** Can easily scale to accommodate increasing call volumes.

Outcome: Anthem reported a significant reduction in call handling times and increased customer satisfaction scores.

Care Management

Care management involves coordinating care to improve health outcomes, particularly for patients with chronic conditions. AI-driven tools are enhancing the ability of payers to manage care more effectively.

Use Case: Predictive Analytics for High-Risk Patients

Predictive analytics can identify patients at high risk of hospitalization or adverse health events, enabling proactive care management.

Example: UnitedHealth Group. UnitedHealth Group uses predictive analytics to identify patients at risk of developing chronic conditions. Their AI system analyzes claims data, electronic health records, and lifestyle information to predict which members are likely to develop conditions like diabetes or heart disease.

Why It Works:

- **Proactive Care:** Enables early intervention to prevent complications.
- **Resource Allocation:** Focuses resources on high-risk patients.
- **Improved Outcomes:** Reduces hospitalizations and improves health outcomes.

Outcome: UnitedHealth Group saw a reduction in hospital admissions and improved management of chronic diseases among its members.

Disease Management

Effective disease management programs are essential for improving patient health and reducing healthcare costs. AI is playing a critical role in enhancing these programs.

Use Case: Personalized Disease Management Plans

AI can create personalized disease management plans by analyzing a patient's medical history, lifestyle, and genetic data.

Example: Humana. Humana developed an AI-driven platform that provides personalized disease management plans for members with diabetes. The platform analyzes various data points, including blood sugar levels, diet, exercise, and medication adherence, to provide tailored advice and reminders.

Why It Works:

- **Personalization:** Tailors recommendations to individual needs.
- **Continuous Monitoring:** Provides real-time feedback and adjustments.
- **Engagement:** Increases patient engagement and adherence to treatment plans.

Outcome: Humana reported improved blood sugar control and increased adherence to treatment plans among its members.

Fraud Detection and Prevention

Fraud detection and prevention are critical for reducing costs and maintaining the integrity of payer operations. AI is significantly enhancing these efforts by identifying patterns and anomalies that indicate fraudulent activities.

Use Case: Machine Learning for Fraud Detection

ML algorithms can analyze vast amounts of data to detect fraudulent claims, reducing financial losses and improving operational efficiency.

Example: Aetna. Aetna implemented an AI-driven fraud detection system that uses ML to analyze claims data and identify patterns indicative of fraud. The system flags suspicious claims for further investigation.

Why It Works:

- **Accuracy:** Detects subtle patterns and anomalies that may indicate fraud.
- **Efficiency:** Automates the detection process, reducing the need for manual review.
- **Real-Time Analysis:** Identifies fraudulent activities quickly, allowing for prompt action.
- **Outcome:** Aetna reported a significant reduction in fraudulent claims and improved efficiency in their fraud detection processes.

Practical Do's and Don'ts for AI in Payer Operations

Do's:

- **Do Involve Stakeholders Early and Often:** Ensure that all stakeholders, including call center staff, care managers, and fraud investigators, are involved in the AI implementation process. Their insights are invaluable.
- **Do Invest in High-Quality Data:** High-quality data is essential for training accurate AI models. Invest in proper data collection, cleaning, and annotation processes.
- **Do Start Small and Scale:** Begin with pilot projects to test AI systems on a small scale. Learn from these pilots before scaling up to full deployment.
- **Do Provide Comprehensive Training:** Ensure that all users are adequately trained on how to use AI tools. This includes technical training and understanding the benefits and limitations of AI.
- **Do Monitor and Refine Continuously:** AI systems require ongoing monitoring and refinement. Establish processes for regular updates and performance assessments.

Don't's:

- **Don't Ignore the Human Element:** AI is a tool to augment human capabilities, not replace them. Ensure that the human element remains central to operations.
- **Don't Skimp on Security:** AI systems often handle sensitive data. Prioritize robust security measures to protect this information.
- **Don't Overrely on Vendors:** While vendors provide valuable technology, develop internal expertise to customize and troubleshoot AI systems effectively.
- **Don't Overpromise:** Set realistic expectations for what AI can achieve. Avoid hyping capabilities that aren't yet feasible.
- **Don't Neglect Ethical Considerations:** Address ethical issues such as bias and fairness proactively. Ensure that AI systems are transparent and accountable.

Conclusion

AI, driven by ML and Generative capabilities, is transforming payer operations from call centers to care management, disease management, and fraud detection. By learning from successful use cases and adhering to practical do's and don'ts, payers can harness AI's power to improve efficiency, enhance patient outcomes, and reduce costs. The future of AI in payer operations is bright, and with the right approach, the possibilities are endless.

Bibliography

Doi, K. (2007). "Computer-aided diagnosis in medical imaging: Historical review, current status and future potential." Computerized Medical Imaging and Graphics, 31(4–5), 198–211. https://doi.org/10.1016/j.compmedimag.2007.02.002

Ferrucci, D., Brown, E., Chu-Carroll, J., Fan, J., Gondek, D., Kalyanpur, A. A., Lally, A., Murdock, J. W., Nyberg, E., Prager, J., Schlaefer, N., & Welty, C. (2010). "Building Watson: An overview of the DeepQA project." AI Magazine, 31(3), 59–79. https://doi.org/10.1609/aimag.v31i3.2303

Krizhevsky, A., Sutskever, I., & Hinton, G. E. (2012). "ImageNet classification with deep convolutional neural networks." Advances in Neural Information Processing Systems, 25, 1097–1105. https://papers.nips.cc/paper/4824-imagenet-classification-with-deep-convolutional-neural-networks

McKinney, S. M., Sieniek, M., Godbole, V., Godwin, J., Antropova, N., Ashrafian, H., Back, T., Chesus, M., Corrado, G. S., Darzi, A., Etemadi, M., Garcia-Vicente, F., Gilbert, F. J., Halling-Brown, M., Hassabis, D., Jansen, S., Karthikesalingam, A., Kelly, C. J., King, D., … Shetty, S. (2020). "International evaluation of an AI system for breast cancer screening." Nature, 577(7788), 89–94. https://doi.org/10.1038/s41586-019-1799-6

Memorial Sloan Kettering Cancer Center. (2012, March 22). "Memorial Sloan-Kettering Cancer Center, IBM to collaborate in applying Watson technology to help oncologists [Press release]." https://www.mskcc.org/news-releases/mskcc-ibm-collaborate-applying-watson-technology-help-oncologists

Moderna, Inc. (2020). "Moderna's work on a potential vaccine against COVID-19." https://www.modernatx.com/modernas-work-potential-vaccine-against-covid-19

Ross, C., & Swetlitz, I. (2017, September 5). "IBM pitched its Watson supercomputer as a revolution in cancer care. It's nowhere close." STAT News. https://www.statnews.com/2017/09/05/watson-ibm-cancer/

Silver, D., Huang, A., Maddison, C. J., Guez, A., Sifre, L., van den Driessche, G., Schrittwieser, J., Antonoglou, I., Panneershelvam, V., Lanctot, M., Dieleman, S., Grewe, D., Nham, J., Kalchbrenner, N., Sutskever, I., Lillicrap, T., Leach, M., Kavukcuoglu, K., Graepel, T., & Hassabis, D. (2016). "Mastering the game of Go with deep neural networks and tree search." Nature, 529(7587), 484–489. https://doi.org/10.1038/nature16961

Chapter 5

AI in Pharmacies and Drug Manufacturing: The New Frontier

Artificial Intelligence (AI) is not only revolutionizing healthcare providers and payers but is also making waves in the pharmacy and drug manufacturing sectors. From optimizing medication management to accelerating drug discovery, AI is enabling breakthroughs that were once the stuff of science fiction. In this chapter, we will explore how Machine Learning (ML) and Generative AI are transforming these sectors, with a special focus on the latest developments in medicine and pharmacy, such as GLP-1 drugs, genetic testing, molecular advancements, and the pioneering efforts of companies like Moderna.

Optimizing Medication Management

Pharmacies are on the frontline of patient care, and AI-driven solutions are enhancing their ability to manage medications

DOI: 10.4324/9781003571407-8

effectively, ensuring patients receive the right drugs at the right time.

Use Case: Predictive Analytics for Inventory Management

AI can optimize inventory management by predicting medication demand based on historical data, seasonal trends, and emerging health issues.

Example: CVS Health. CVS Health implemented an AI-driven inventory management system that uses predictive analytics to forecast medication demand. The system analyzes prescription trends, flu season data, and other factors to ensure that pharmacies are well-stocked with necessary medications.

Why It Works:

- **Accuracy:** Predicts demand with high accuracy, reducing stockouts and overstock.
- **Efficiency:** Streamlines inventory processes, saving time and resources.
- **Customer Satisfaction:** Ensures medications are available when patients need them.

Outcome: CVS Health reported a reduction in medication shortages and an increase in customer satisfaction due to improved availability of medications.

Use Case: Personalized Medication Adherence Programs

AI can create personalized medication adherence programs, reminding patients to take their medications and tracking their compliance.

Example: PillPack (by Amazon). PillPack, an online pharmacy acquired by Amazon, uses AI to create personalized medication adherence programs. The AI system sends reminders to patients to take their medications and tracks adherence, providing alerts to caregivers if doses are missed.

Why It Works:

- **Personalization:** Tailors reminders and adherence plans to individual patient needs.
- **Engagement:** Keeps patients engaged and informed about their medication schedules.
- **Support:** Provides caregivers with real-time adherence data, allowing for timely interventions.

Outcome: PillPack reported improved medication adherence rates among its customers, leading to better health outcomes and reduced hospital readmissions.

Accelerating Drug Discovery

AI is revolutionizing drug discovery, significantly reducing the time and cost required to bring new drugs to market. By analyzing vast amounts of data, AI can identify promising drug candidates, predict their efficacy, and optimize clinical trials.

Use Case: Generative AI for Drug Discovery

Generative AI models can create new drug compounds by analyzing existing drugs and predicting their interactions with various biological targets.

Example: Moderna. Moderna has been a pioneer in leveraging AI for drug discovery. During the COVID-19 pandemic, Moderna stood up over 400 Generative Pre-trained Transformers (GPTs) to accelerate the development of its mRNA vaccine. These AI models analyzed vast datasets of genetic information, predicted the most effective mRNA sequences, and optimized the vaccine development process.

Why It Works:

- **Speed:** Rapidly generates and tests new drug compounds.
- **Accuracy:** Predicts the efficacy and safety of new drugs with high accuracy.
- **Efficiency:** Reduces the time and cost associated with traditional drug discovery methods.

Outcome: Moderna's use of AI allowed for the swift development and approval of its COVID-19 vaccine, demonstrating the potential of AI to transform drug discovery.

Genetic Testing and Personalized Medicine

AI is at the forefront of genetic testing and personalized medicine, enabling more precise diagnoses and tailored treatments based on an individual's genetic makeup.

Use Case: AI-Driven Genetic Testing

AI can analyze genetic data to identify mutations and predict an individual's risk of developing certain diseases. This information can be used to create personalized treatment plans.

Example: 23andMe. 23andMe, a direct-to-consumer genetic testing company, uses AI to analyze genetic data and provide customers with personalized health reports. These reports include information on genetic predispositions to various conditions and recommendations for lifestyle changes and medical interventions.

Why It Works:

- **Personalization:** Provides individualized health insights based on genetic data.
- **Proactivity:** Enables early detection and prevention of diseases.
- **Engagement:** Empowers individuals to take control of their health.

Outcome: 23andMe has helped millions of customers gain insights into their genetic health, leading to increased awareness and proactive health management.

Use Case: AI for Personalized Cancer Treatment

AI can analyze genetic and molecular data to develop personalized cancer treatment plans, improving outcomes and reducing side effects.

Example: Foundation Medicine. Foundation Medicine uses AI to analyze tumor genetics and identify personalized treatment options for cancer patients. Their AI platform integrates genomic data with clinical trial information to recommend targeted therapies.

Why It Works:

- **Precision:** Identifies the most effective treatments based on genetic mutations.
- **Efficiency:** Streamlines the process of matching patients with clinical trials.
- **Outcomes:** Improves treatment efficacy and reduces adverse effects.

Outcome: Foundation Medicine's AI-driven approach has led to more effective cancer treatments and improved patient outcomes.

AI in GLP-1 Drugs and Other Molecular Advancements

Glucagon-like peptide-1 (GLP-1) drugs and other molecular advancements are at the cutting edge of medical science. AI is playing a crucial role in the development and optimization of these drugs.

Use Case: AI in GLP-1 Drug Development

GLP-1 drugs are a class of medications used to treat type 2 diabetes and obesity. AI is being used to enhance the development and effectiveness of these drugs.

Example: Novo Nordisk. Novo Nordisk, a leader in diabetes care, uses AI to develop and optimize GLP-1 drugs. Their AI platform analyzes clinical trial data, patient responses, and molecular structures to identify the most promising GLP-1 drug candidates and optimize their formulations.

Why It Works:

- **Efficiency:** Accelerates the drug development process.
- **Precision:** Optimizes drug formulations for better efficacy and fewer side effects.
- **Innovation:** Identifies new drug candidates with novel mechanisms of action.

Outcome: Novo Nordisk's use of AI has led to the development of highly effective GLP-1 drugs, improving outcomes for patients with type 2 diabetes and obesity.

Use Case: AI in Genetic and Molecular Advancements

AI is driving advancements in genetic and molecular medicine, enabling the development of new therapies and enhancing our understanding of complex biological processes.

Example: Insilico Medicine. Insilico Medicine uses AI to design new molecules for drug development. Their AI platform analyzes biological data to identify potential drug targets and generate new molecules that interact with these targets.

Why It Works:

- **Innovation:** Creates novel molecules that may not be discovered through traditional methods.
- **Speed:** Accelerates the drug development process.
- **Precision:** Ensures that molecules have the desired therapeutic properties.

Outcome: Insilico Medicine has successfully developed several drug candidates, demonstrating the potential of AI-driven molecular design.

Practical Do's and Don'ts for AI in Pharmacies and Drug Manufacturing

Do's:

- **Do Invest in High-Quality Data:** High-quality data is essential for training accurate AI models. Invest in proper data collection, cleaning, and annotation processes.
- **Do Collaborate with Experts:** Collaborate with healthcare and pharmaceutical experts to ensure that AI systems meet industry standards and address real-world challenges.
- **Do Start Small and Scale:** Begin with pilot projects to test AI systems on a small scale. Learn from these pilots before scaling up to full deployment.

- **Do Prioritize Security:** Ensure that AI systems handling sensitive genetic and health data are secure and comply with regulatory standards.
- **Do Continuously Monitor and Improve:** AI systems require ongoing monitoring and refinement. Establish processes for regular updates and performance assessments.

Don'ts:

- **Don't Overlook the Human Element:** AI is a tool to augment human capabilities, not replace them. Ensure that the human element remains central to operations.
- **Don't Ignore Ethical Considerations:** Address ethical issues such as bias and fairness proactively. Ensure that AI systems are transparent and accountable.
- **Don't Skimp on Training:** Provide comprehensive training to all users of AI systems, ensuring they understand how to use the tools effectively.
- **Don't Overpromise:** Set realistic expectations for what AI can achieve. Avoid hyping capabilities that aren't yet feasible.
- **Don't Neglect Interoperability:** Ensure that AI systems can integrate with existing infrastructure and other technologies used in pharmacies and drug manufacturing.

Conclusion

AI, driven by ML and Generative capabilities, is transforming pharmacies and drug manufacturing. From optimizing medication management and accelerating drug discovery to enabling personalized medicine and molecular advancements, AI is driving unprecedented innovations. By learning from successful use cases and adhering to practical do's and don'ts, pharmacies and drug manufacturers can harness AI's power to improve patient outcomes, streamline operations, and drive innovation.

The future of AI in pharmacies and drug manufacturing is bright, and with the right approach, the possibilities are endless. As the industry continues to adopt and integrate AI technologies, we can expect even more groundbreaking advancements that will shape the future of medicine. The integration of AI not only promises efficiency and innovation but also holds the potential to revolutionize how we approach healthcare, making it more personalized, proactive, and precise.

Bibliography

23andMe, Inc. (n.d.). "Personalized genetic reports." https://www.23andme.com/dna-reports-list/

Amazon Pharmacy. (n.d.). "PillPack by Amazon Pharmacy." https://pharmacy.amazon.com/pillpack

Anthem, Inc. (2020). "Anthem link and AI in healthcare — The future of healthcare is digital." https://www.anthembluecross.com/employer/the-benefits-guide/the-future-of-healthcare-is-digital

Doi, K. (2007). "Computer-aided diagnosis in medical imaging: Historical review, current status and future potential." Computerized Medical Imaging and Graphics, 31(4–5), 198–211. https://doi.org/10.1016/j.compmedimag.2007.02.002 — full text: https://pmc.ncbi.nlm.nih.gov/articles/PMC1955762/

Ferrucci, D., Brown, E., Chu-Carroll, J., Fan, J., Gondek, D., Kalyanpur, A. A., Lally, A., Murdock, J. W., Nyberg, E., Prager, J., Schlaefer, N., & Welty, C. (2010). "Building Watson: An overview of the DeepQA project." AI Magazine, 31(3), 59–79. https://doi.org/10.1609/aimag.v31i3.2303

Foundation Medicine, Inc. (n.d.). "FoundationOne CDx." https://www.foundationmedicine.com/test/foundationone-cdx

Krizhevsky, A., Sutskever, I., & Hinton, G. E. (2012). "ImageNet classification with deep convolutional neural networks." Advances in Neural Information Processing Systems, 25, 1097–1105. https://papers.nips.cc/paper/4824-imagenet-classification-with-deep-convolutional-neural-networks

Silver, D., Huang, A., Maddison, C. J., Guez, A., Sifre, L., van den Driessche, G., Schrittwieser, J., Antonoglou, I., Panneershelvam, V., Lanctot, M., Dieleman, S., Grewe, D., Nham, J., Kalchbrenner, N., Sutskever, I., Lillicrap, T., Leach, M., Kavukcuoglu, K., Graepel, T., & Hassabis, D. (2016). "Mastering the game of go with deep neural networks and tree search." Nature, 529(7587), 484–489. https://doi.org/10.1038/nature16961 — https://www.nature.com/articles/nature16961

McKinney, S. M., Sieniek, M., Godbole, V., Godwin, J., Antropova, N., Ashrafian, H., Back, T., Chesus, M., Corrado, G. S., Darzi, A., Etemadi, M., Garcia-Vicente, F., Gilbert, F. J., Halling-Brown, M., Hassabis, D., Jansen, S., Karthikesalingam, A., Kelly, C. J., King, D., … Shetty, S. (2020). "International evaluation of an AI system for breast cancer screening." Nature, 577(7788), 89–94. https://doi.org/10.1038/s41586-019-1799-6 — https://www.nature.com/articles/s41586-019-1799-6

Memorial Sloan Kettering Cancer Center. (2012, March 22). "Memorial Sloan-Kettering Cancer Center, IBM to collaborate in applying Watson technology to help oncologists [Press release]." https://www.mskcc.org/news-releases/mskcc-ibm-collaborate-applying-watson-technology-help-oncologists

Moderna, Inc. (2020). "Moderna's work on a potential vaccine against COVID-19." https://www.modernatx.com/modernas-work-potential-vaccine-against-covid-19

UnitedHealthcare. (2021, July 8). "UnitedHealthcare introduces the use of predictive analytics to expand its capabilities to address social determinants of health [Press release]." https://www.unitedhealthgroup.com/newsroom/2021/2021-7-8-uhc-predictive-analytics-social-determinants-health.html

Zhavoronkov, A., Ivanenkov, Y. A., Aliper, A., Veselov, M. S., Aladinskiy, V. A., Aladinskaya, A. V., Terentiev, V. A., Polykovskiy, D. A., Kuznetsov, M. D., Asadulaev, A., Volkov, Y., Zholus, A., Shayakhmetov, R. R., Zhebrak, A., Minaeva, L. I., Zagribelnyy, B. A., Lee, L. H., Soll, R., Madge, D., … Aspuru-Guzik, A. (2019). "Deep learning enables rapid identification of potent DDR1 kinase inhibitors." Nature Biotechnology, 37(9), 1038–1040. https://doi.org/10.1038/s41587-019-0224-x — Insilico Medicine: https://insilico.com/

Chapter 6

Unleashing Talent: Winning the AI Talent War

As AI continues to revolutionize the healthcare industry, the demand for skilled professionals who can develop, implement, and manage AI systems has skyrocketed. The fierce competition for AI talent has made it one of the most significant challenges for organizations looking to leverage AI effectively. This chapter will explore the strategies for attracting, retaining, and developing AI talent, along with real-world examples and practical do's and don'ts.

The Fierce Competition for AI Talent

The rapid advancement of AI technologies has created a significant talent gap. Companies across various industries, not just healthcare, are vying for a limited pool of AI experts. This competition has driven up salaries and benefits, making it even more challenging for healthcare organizations to attract top talent.

DOI: 10.4324/9781003571407-9

The AI Talent Shortage

The shortage of AI talent is a well-documented issue. According to a report by the World Economic Forum, the demand for AI skills has more than doubled over the past few years, while the supply has struggled to keep pace. This imbalance has created a highly competitive job market where top talent is in high demand.

Example: Google DeepMind. Google DeepMind, known for its groundbreaking AI research, has faced challenges in attracting and retaining top talent despite its reputation and resources. The competition from other tech giants and the lucrative offers from startups have made it difficult to maintain a stable workforce.

Why It Works:

- **Reputation:** Google's reputation attracts top talent.
- **Resources:** DeepMind's resources enable cutting-edge research.
- **Challenges:** High-profile projects and challenges keep talent engaged.

Outcome: Despite the challenges, DeepMind continues to attract and retain top talent by offering competitive compensation, challenging projects, and opportunities for professional growth.

Why Traditional Recruitment Methods Fail

Traditional recruitment methods often fall short when it comes to attracting AI talent. Posting job listings on traditional platforms and relying on standard recruitment processes do not resonate with the unique needs and interests of AI professionals.

The Limitations of Traditional Recruitment

Traditional recruitment methods are often too slow and bureaucratic to compete in the fast-paced AI job market. AI professionals seek opportunities for innovation, impact, and career growth, which are not always communicated effectively through conventional channels.

Example: A Leading Healthcare Provider. A leading healthcare provider struggled to fill AI positions using traditional recruitment methods. The lengthy hiring process and lack of clarity about the role's impact on patient care deterred potential candidates.

Why It Didn't Work:

- **Slow Process:** Lengthy hiring processes are a turn-off for top talent.
- **Lack of Clarity:** Poor communication of the role's impact and opportunities.
- **Generic Listings:** Job listings failed to stand out in a competitive market.

Outcome: The healthcare provider revised its recruitment strategy, emphasizing the role's impact on patient care and streamlining the hiring process to attract top AI talent.

Building an AI Team against the Odds

To win the AI talent war, companies must implement innovative strategies. Developing a strong employer brand, engaging in proactive talent sourcing, and fostering a collaborative and inclusive culture are essential steps.

Developing a Strong Employer Brand

A strong employer brand that highlights the company's commitment to innovation, professional growth, and positive impact is crucial for attracting AI talent.

Example: Microsoft has built a strong employer brand by emphasizing its commitment to innovation and impact. The company's AI for Good initiative, which uses AI to address global challenges, has attracted top talent passionate about making a difference.

Why It Works:

- **Innovation:** Emphasizes the company's focus on cutting-edge technology.
- **Impact:** Attracts talent motivated by the potential to make a positive impact.
- **Growth:** Offers opportunities for professional development and growth.

Outcome: Microsoft's strong employer brand has helped it attract and retain top AI talent, enabling the company to stay at the forefront of AI innovation.

Engaging in Proactive Talent Sourcing

Proactive talent sourcing involves building relationships with potential candidates before they are actively looking for a job. This approach can include participating in AI conferences, collaborating with universities, and using social media to connect with AI professionals.

Example: Facebook AI Research (FAIR). FAIR engages in proactive talent sourcing by participating in AI conferences, publishing research, and collaborating with academic institutions. This strategy helps them identify and attract top talent early in their careers.

Why It Works:

- **Early Engagement:** Identifies talent before they enter the job market.
- **Networking:** Builds relationships with potential candidates.
- **Visibility:** Increases the company's visibility in the AI community.

Outcome: FAIR's proactive talent sourcing has enabled them to build a strong pipeline of AI talent, ensuring a steady influx of skilled professionals.

Creating a Collaborative and Inclusive Culture

A collaborative and inclusive culture is essential for retaining AI talent. AI professionals value environments where they can collaborate with peers, share ideas, and feel included.

Example: IBM Watson Health. IBM Watson Health fosters a collaborative and inclusive culture by encouraging cross-functional teams, hosting hackathons, and promoting diversity and inclusion initiatives.

Why It Works:

- **Collaboration:** Encourages the exchange of ideas and innovation.
- **Inclusion:** Ensures all team members feel valued and included.
- **Engagement:** Increases employee engagement and satisfaction.

Outcome: IBM Watson Health's collaborative and inclusive culture has resulted in higher employee retention rates and a more innovative work environment.

Practical Do's and Don'ts for Building an AI Team

Do's

- **Do Develop a Strong Employer Brand:** Highlight your company's commitment to innovation, professional growth, and positive impact to attract top AI talent.
- **Do Engage in Proactive Talent Sourcing:** Build relationships with potential candidates through conferences, academic collaborations, and social media.
- **Do Foster a Collaborative and Inclusive Culture:** Create an environment where AI professionals can collaborate, share ideas, and feel included.
- **Do Invest in Continuous Learning and Development:** Provide opportunities for professional growth through training, workshops, and advanced education programs.
- **Do Offer Competitive Compensation and Benefits:** Ensure that your compensation packages are competitive with industry standards to attract and retain top talent.

Don'ts

- **Don't Rely Solely on Traditional Recruitment Methods:** Move beyond conventional hiring practices to attract AI talent through innovative strategies.
- **Don't Ignore the Importance of Culture:** A toxic or uninspiring work environment will drive away top talent. Prioritize a positive and inclusive culture.
- **Don't Overlook the Need for Clear Communication:** Clearly communicate the role's impact, opportunities for growth, and the company's vision to potential candidates.
- **Don't Skimp on Resources:** Provide the necessary tools, technologies, and support for your AI team to succeed.

- **Don't Underestimate the Power of Networking:** Build and maintain a strong network within the AI community to stay connected with potential talent.

Conclusion

Winning the AI talent war requires a strategic approach that goes beyond traditional recruitment methods. By developing a strong employer brand, engaging in proactive talent sourcing, fostering a collaborative and inclusive culture, and providing continuous learning opportunities, companies can attract and retain top AI talent. The future of AI in healthcare depends on the skills and creativity of these professionals, and with the right strategies, organizations can build a world-class AI team capable of driving innovation and improving patient outcomes.

Bibliography

Doi, K. (2007). "Computer-aided diagnosis in medical imaging: Historical review, current status and future potential." Computerized Medical Imaging and Graphics, 31(4–5), 198–211.

Ferrucci, D., et al. (2010). "Building Watson: An overview of the DeepQA project." AI Magazine, 31(3), 59–79.

IBM Watson Health. (2013). "Watson for oncology." Retrieved from IBM Watson Health

Krizhevsky, A., Sutskever, I., & Hinton, G. E. (2012). "Imagenet classification with deep convolutional neural networks." Advances in Neural Information Processing Systems, 25, 1097–1105.

McKinney, S. M., et al. (2020). "International evaluation of an AI system for breast cancer screening." Nature, 577, 89–94.

Silver, D., et al. (2016). "Mastering the game of Go with deep neural networks and tree search." Nature, 529(7587), 484–489.

Chapter 7

Provocative Tools: Beyond the AI Sales Pitch

Artificial Intelligence (AI) has become the hottest buzzword in the healthcare industry. From flashy presentations at conferences to slick marketing brochures, AI tools and platforms are being touted as the silver bullet for all healthcare woes. However, cutting through the hype and understanding the true value of these tools are crucial for making informed decisions. This chapter will expose the vendor hype, provide criteria for evaluating AI tools, and share real-world evaluations to help healthcare organizations navigate the crowded AI marketplace.

Exposing the Vendor Hype

The promise of AI is alluring, but the reality often falls short of the marketing claims. Vendors are eager to sell their AI solutions, sometimes overselling their capabilities and underdelivering on results.

DOI: 10.4324/9781003571407-10

The Hype vs. Reality

AI vendors often promise revolutionary results with minimal effort, creating unrealistic expectations. While AI has the potential to transform healthcare, achieving meaningful results requires a significant investment in time, resources, and expertise.

Example: Watson for Oncology. IBM Watson for Oncology was marketed as a groundbreaking AI tool that could assist oncologists in developing personalized cancer treatment plans. However, several studies and real-world implementations revealed that Watson's recommendations were often inconsistent with those of human experts and, in some cases, outdated (Ross & Swetlitz, 2017).

Why It Fell Short:

- **Data Limitations:** Incomplete or outdated training data.
- **Integration Challenges:** Difficulty integrating with existing healthcare systems.
- **Overhyped Expectations:** Marketing claims that did not align with the tool's actual capabilities.

Outcome: Watson for Oncology faced significant criticism, highlighting the importance of validating AI tools before widespread adoption.

Criteria for Cutting through Marketing BS

Evaluating AI tools requires a critical approach. Here are some criteria to help healthcare organizations distinguish between genuinely valuable tools and overhyped products.

Criteria for Evaluation:

1. **Data Quality and Relevance:** Assess the quality and relevance of the data used to train the AI model.

High-quality, diverse, and up-to-date data are essential for accurate and reliable AI predictions.

2. **Transparency and Explainability:** Ensure the AI tool provides transparent and explainable results. Healthcare professionals need to understand how the AI arrives at its conclusions to trust and effectively use the tool.
3. **Integration and Compatibility:** Evaluate how well the AI tool integrates with existing healthcare systems, such as Electronic Health Records (EHRs). Seamless integration is crucial for workflow efficiency.
4. **Regulatory Compliance:** Confirm that the AI tool complies with relevant healthcare regulations and standards, such as HIPAA in the United States, to ensure patient data privacy and security.
5. **Clinical Validation:** Look for evidence of clinical validation through peer-reviewed studies, real-world case studies, and endorsements from reputable healthcare institutions.
6. **Vendor Support and Training:** Consider the level of support and training provided by the vendor. Effective implementation and ongoing use of AI tools require robust support and training programs.

Real-World Evaluations of AI Technologies

To illustrate how these criteria can be applied, let's examine real-world evaluations of AI technologies in healthcare.

Example 1 Zebra Medical Vision

Zebra Medical Vision offers AI-powered imaging analytics to assist radiologists in detecting medical conditions from X-rays, CT scans, and MRIs.

Evaluation:

- **Data Quality and Relevance:** Zebra Medical Vision's algorithms are trained on a vast dataset of medical images from diverse sources, ensuring high-quality and relevant data.
- **Transparency and Explainability:** The tool provides explainable results, allowing radiologists to understand the AI's decision-making process.
- **Integration and Compatibility:** It integrates seamlessly with major Picture Archiving and Communication Systems (PACS), facilitating easy adoption.
- **Regulatory Compliance:** The tool is FDA-cleared and CE-marked, ensuring compliance with regulatory standards.
- **Clinical Validation:** Zebra Medical Vision has published multiple peer-reviewed studies validating the accuracy of its AI algorithms.
- **Vendor Support and Training:** The company offers comprehensive support and training programs to ensure effective use of the tool.

Outcome: Zebra Medical Vision has been successfully adopted by numerous healthcare providers, enhancing diagnostic accuracy and efficiency in medical imaging.

Example 2 Aidoc

Aidoc provides AI solutions for radiology, offering tools to detect acute abnormalities in medical imaging.

Evaluation:

- **Data Quality and Relevance:** Aidoc's AI models are trained on a large dataset of annotated medical images, ensuring robust performance.
- **Transparency and Explainability:** The platform offers explainable AI, helping radiologists understand and trust the results.

- **Integration and Compatibility:** Aidoc's tools are designed to integrate with existing radiology workflows and PACS.
- **Regulatory Compliance:** The AI solutions are FDA-cleared and CE-marked, meeting regulatory requirements.
- **Clinical Validation:** Aidoc has demonstrated its effectiveness through multiple clinical studies and real-world implementations.
- **Vendor Support and Training:** The company provides strong support and training to facilitate smooth adoption and use.

Outcome: Aidoc's AI tools have been widely adopted, improving the detection of critical findings in radiology and enhancing patient outcomes.

Practical Do's and Don'ts for Evaluating AI Tools

Do's

- **Do Conduct Thorough Due Diligence:** Investigate the AI tool's data quality, clinical validation, and regulatory compliance before making a decision.
- **Do Engage Clinical Staff:** Involve healthcare professionals in the evaluation process to ensure the tool meets clinical needs and can be seamlessly integrated into workflows.
- **Do Request Demonstrations and Trials:** Request live demonstrations and trial periods to evaluate the tool's performance in your specific healthcare environment.
- **Do Prioritize Transparency and Explainability:** Choose AI tools that offer transparent and explainable results to build trust and facilitate effective use.

- **Do Consider Vendor Support:** Ensure the vendor provides comprehensive support and training programs to aid in the successful implementation and ongoing use of the AI tool.

Don'ts

- **Don't Fall for Overhyped Claims:** Be wary of marketing claims that sound too good to be true. Look for evidence and clinical validation to back up the tool's capabilities.
- **Don't Ignore Integration Challenges:** Evaluate how well the AI tool integrates with your existing systems to avoid disruptions in workflows.
- **Don't Neglect Data Security:** Ensure the AI tool complies with data privacy and security regulations to protect patient information.
- **Don't Overlook the Importance of Clinical Validation:** Verify that the AI tool has been clinically validated through peer-reviewed studies and real-world implementations.
- **Don't Skimp on Training:** Invest in comprehensive training for your staff to ensure they are equipped to use the AI tool effectively.

Conclusion

AI tools hold tremendous potential to transform healthcare, but cutting through the vendor hype and making informed decisions is essential. By applying critical evaluation criteria and learning from real-world examples, healthcare organizations can identify genuinely valuable AI tools that enhance patient care, improve efficiency, and drive innovation.

The future of AI in healthcare is promising, and with the right tools, organizations can unlock its full potential.

Bibliography

Aidoc. (n.d.). “Radiology AI imaging — Faster, smarter care.” https://www.aidoc.com/solutions/radiology/

Nano-X Imaging Ltd. (2021, November 8). “Nanox completes merger with Zebra Medical Vision, Ltd., re-brand as Nanox.AI, and acquisition of MDWEB, LLC., and USARAD Holdings, Inc. [Press release].” https://investors.nanox.vision/news-releases/news-release-details/nanox-completes-merger-zebra-medical-vision-ltd-re-brand-nanoxai/

Ross, C., & Swetlitz, I. (2017, September 5). “IBM pitched its Watson supercomputer as a revolution in cancer care. It's nowhere close.” STAT News. https://www.statnews.com/2017/09/05/watson-ibm-cancer/

U.S. Food and Drug Administration. (2021, January). “Artificial intelligence/machine learning (AI/ML)-based software as a medical device (SaMD) action plan.” https://www.fda.gov/media/145022/download — press release: https://www.fda.gov/news-events/press-announcements/fda-releases-artificial-intelligencemachine-learning-action-plan

Chapter 8

Transformative Implementation: Embrace Fail Fast, Learn Faster

The rapid evolution of Artificial Intelligence (AI) in healthcare demands not only cutting-edge technology but also a robust and flexible implementation strategy. Embracing a "fail fast, learn faster" approach is crucial to harnessing AI's full potential. This chapter will explore the importance of iterative development, provide real-world case studies of quick pivots and rapid learning, and offer practical do's and don'ts for successful AI implementation.

Embracing Failure as a Crucial Part of AI Development

In the world of AI, failure is not just an option – it's a necessity. The iterative process of trial, error, and adjustment is

DOI: 10.4324/9781003571407-11

fundamental to developing effective AI solutions. By accepting that failures will happen and learning from them quickly, healthcare organizations can accelerate their AI journey and achieve better results.

The "Fail Fast, Learn Faster" Philosophy

The "fail fast, learn faster" philosophy encourages rapid experimentation and iteration. This approach is particularly well-suited to AI, where models and algorithms often need to be refined and adjusted based on real-world data and feedback.

Example: Google Health's AI for Diabetic Retinopathy. Google Health developed an AI system to detect diabetic retinopathy, a leading cause of blindness. Initial trials in India faced challenges due to varying image quality and differences in clinical practices. Instead of abandoning the project, Google Health iterated on its model, incorporating feedback from local clinicians and improving the system's robustness (Gulshan et al., 2016).

Why It Works:

- **Rapid Feedback:** Allows for quick identification of issues and areas for improvement.
- **Adaptability:** Enables the AI system to adapt to different environments and data conditions.
- **Continuous Improvement:** Fosters a culture of ongoing learning and development.

Outcome: Google Health's refined AI system achieved high accuracy in detecting diabetic retinopathy and is now used in multiple countries, demonstrating the power of iterative development.

Iterative Development over Big Bang Approaches

A big bang approach to AI implementation – where a comprehensive solution is deployed all at once – often leads to significant risks and failures. Iterative development, however, allows for gradual improvements and mitigates the risks associated with large-scale deployments.

Case Study: Mayo Clinic's AI-Driven Predictive Analytics

Mayo Clinic adopted an iterative approach to implementing AI-driven predictive analytics for patient care. Instead of rolling out a comprehensive solution immediately, they started with a pilot project focusing on predicting patient readmissions.

Why It Worked:

- **Pilot Projects:** Starting with a pilot project allowed Mayo Clinic to test the AI system on a smaller scale and gather valuable feedback.
- **Scalability:** Successful pilot projects provided a blueprint for scaling the AI system across the organization.
- **Stakeholder Buy-In:** Iterative development helped secure buy-in from clinicians and staff, who saw the system's benefits firsthand.

Outcome: Mayo Clinic successfully scaled its AI-driven predictive analytics system, leading to reduced readmission rates and improved patient outcomes.

Case Studies of Quick Pivots and Rapid Learning

Learning from real-world examples of quick pivots and rapid learning can provide valuable insights into effective AI implementation.

Case Study: Stanford Medicine's AI for Radiology

Stanford Medicine developed an AI system to assist radiologists in detecting pneumonia from chest X-rays. Initial deployments revealed discrepancies between the AI's predictions and radiologists' diagnoses. Instead of discontinuing the project, Stanford Medicine iterated on the AI model, refining its algorithms and incorporating feedback from radiologists.

Why It Worked:

- **Collaboration:** Worked closely with radiologists to understand their needs and improve the AI system.
- **Continuous Learning:** Updated the AI model regularly based on new data and feedback.
- **Real-World Testing:** Deployed the AI system in real-world settings to validate its performance.

Outcome: Stanford Medicine's AI system achieved high accuracy and became a valuable tool for radiologists, highlighting the importance of continuous learning and collaboration.

Practical Do's and Don'ts for AI Implementation

Do's:

- **Do Start with Pilot Projects:** Begin with small-scale pilot projects to test AI systems and gather feedback before scaling up.
- **Do Embrace Iterative Development:** Use an iterative approach to continuously refine and improve AI systems based on real-world data and feedback.
- **Do Engage Stakeholders:** Involve clinicians, staff, and patients in the development and implementation process to ensure the AI system meets their needs.

- **Do Prioritize Transparency:** Be transparent about the capabilities and limitations of AI systems, and communicate openly about challenges and improvements.
- **Do Invest in Training and Support:** Provide comprehensive training and support to ensure that users can effectively operate and benefit from AI systems.

Don'ts:

- **Don't Expect Perfection from the Start:** AI systems often require refinement and improvement. Don't expect them to be perfect from the beginning.
- **Don't Overlook the Importance of Data Quality:** High-quality data is essential for training accurate AI models. Ensure that data used for training is clean, relevant, and diverse.
- **Don't Neglect Ethical Considerations:** Address ethical issues such as bias and fairness proactively to ensure that AI systems are transparent and equitable.
- **Don't Ignore Feedback:** Actively seek and incorporate feedback from users to improve AI systems continuously.
- **Don't Skimp on Monitoring and Evaluation:** Regularly monitor and evaluate AI systems to ensure they are performing as expected and making a positive impact.

Conclusion

Embracing a "fail fast, learn faster" approach is crucial for successful AI implementation in healthcare. By focusing on iterative development, engaging stakeholders, and prioritizing transparency, organizations can overcome challenges and harness AI's full potential. The case studies of Google Health, Mayo Clinic, Babylon Health, and Stanford Medicine demonstrate the power of rapid learning and adaptation in achieving transformative results. By following the practical do's and don'ts outlined in the chapter, healthcare organizations can navigate the complexities of AI implementation and drive meaningful improvements in patient care and operational efficiency.

Bibliography

Gulshan, V., Peng, L., Coram, M., Stumpe, M. C., Wu, D., Narayanaswamy, A., Venugopalan, S., Widner, K., Madams, T., Cuadros, J., Kim, R., Raman, R., Nelson, P. C., Mega, J. L., & Webster, D. R. (2016). "Development and validation of a deep learning algorithm for detection of diabetic retinopathy in retinal fundus photographs." JAMA, 316(22), 2402–2410. https://doi.org/10.1001/jama.2016.17216

Mayo Clinic Platform. (n.d.). "Mayo clinic platform — Transforming healthcare through data and AI." https://www.mayoclinicplatform.org/

Ross, C., & Swetlitz, I. (2017, September 5). "IBM pitched its Watson supercomputer as a revolution in cancer care. It's nowhere close." STAT News. https://www.statnews.com/2017/09/05/watson-ibm-cancer/

Stanford Center for Artificial Intelligence in Medicine and Imaging (AIMI). (n.d.). "Stanford AIMI." https://aimi.stanford.edu/

III CHALLENGES AND CONSIDERATIONS

Chapter 9

AI Ethics Unveiled: Confronting the Dark Side

Artificial Intelligence (AI) has the potential to revolutionize healthcare, but with great power comes great responsibility. As healthcare organizations increasingly rely on AI, it is crucial to address the ethical considerations that come with it. From bias and fairness to patient privacy and data security, this chapter will delve into the uncomfortable truths about AI ethics and provide strategies for making ethics a core priority.

Confronting Bias and Fairness

AI systems are only as good as the data they are trained on. If the data is biased, the AI system will likely perpetuate those biases, leading to unfair and potentially harmful outcomes.

DOI: 10.4324/9781003571407-13

The Problem of Bias in AI

Bias in AI can arise from various sources, including historical data, sampling errors, and algorithmic design. These biases can lead to disparities in healthcare outcomes, particularly for marginalized and vulnerable populations.

Example: Algorithmic Bias in Healthcare. A study published in Science in 2019 found that an algorithm widely used in U.S. hospitals to allocate healthcare resources was biased against Black patients. The algorithm underestimated the health risks of Black patients compared to white patients, leading to unequal access to care (Obermeyer et al., 2019).

Why It Matters:

- **Health Disparities:** Bias in AI can exacerbate existing health disparities.
- **Trust:** Bias undermines trust in AI systems and healthcare providers.
- **Ethical Concerns:** Unfair treatment based on biased AI decisions raises significant ethical issues.

Outcome: The study prompted a re-evaluation of the algorithm and highlighted the need for greater scrutiny and correction of biases in AI systems.

Addressing Bias and Ensuring Fairness

To ensure that AI systems are fair and unbiased, healthcare organizations must implement robust strategies for identifying, mitigating, and monitoring bias.

Strategies for Mitigating Bias:

1. **Diverse Datasets:** Ensure that training data is representative of the population the AI system will serve.

This includes collecting data from diverse demographic groups and geographic regions.

2. **Bias Audits:** Conduct regular bias audits to identify and address biases in AI models. These audits should involve analyzing the performance of AI systems across different demographic groups.
3. **Algorithmic Transparency:** Promote transparency in AI algorithms by providing clear explanations of how they work and the factors they consider in decision-making.
4. **Stakeholder Involvement:** Involve diverse stakeholders, including patients, clinicians, and ethicists, in the development and evaluation of AI systems to ensure multiple perspectives are considered.
5. **Continuous Monitoring:** Implement continuous monitoring processes to detect and correct biases as the AI system operates in real-world settings.

Patient Privacy and Data Security

AI relies on vast amounts of data, raising significant concerns about patient privacy and data security. Ensuring that AI systems comply with regulations and protect patient information is crucial.

The Challenge of Data Privacy

AI systems often require access to sensitive patient data, which must be protected to prevent unauthorized access and breaches. Compliance with regulations such as the Health Insurance Portability and Accountability Act (HIPAA) is essential.

Example: Mayo Clinic and Google. In 2019, the Mayo Clinic partnered with Google to develop AI tools for healthcare while ensuring data privacy and security. The collaboration involved strict adherence to privacy standards and advanced encryption techniques to protect patient data.

Why It Matters:

- **Patient Trust:** Ensuring data privacy is crucial for maintaining patient trust.
- **Legal Compliance:** Non-compliance with data privacy regulations can result in legal consequences and financial penalties.
- **Ethical Responsibility:** Protecting patient data is an ethical obligation for healthcare organizations.

Outcome: The partnership demonstrated that it is possible to leverage AI for healthcare advancements while maintaining robust data privacy and security standards.

Strategies for Ensuring Data Privacy and Security

To protect patient data and ensure compliance with regulations, healthcare organizations should implement comprehensive data privacy and security measures.

Best Practices for Data Privacy and Security:

1. **Data Encryption:** Use advanced encryption techniques to protect data both in transit and at rest.
2. **Access Controls:** Implement strict access controls to ensure that only authorized personnel can access sensitive data.
3. **Anonymization:** Anonymize patient data whenever possible to minimize the risk of re-identification.
4. **Regular Audits:** Conduct regular security audits to identify vulnerabilities and ensure compliance with data privacy regulations.

5. **Patient Consent:** Obtain informed consent from patients for the use of their data in AI systems, clearly explaining how their data will be used and protected.

Ethical AI Development

Developing ethical AI systems requires a commitment to transparency, accountability, and fairness throughout the development process.

The Role of Ethical Guidelines

Ethical guidelines provide a framework for developing and deploying AI systems responsibly. These guidelines should be integrated into every stage of AI development, from data collection to model deployment.

Example: Ethical AI Guidelines by the World Health Organization (WHO). The WHO has developed ethical guidelines for AI in healthcare, emphasizing principles such as transparency, accountability, inclusiveness, and fairness. These guidelines serve as a roadmap for organizations to develop AI systems that prioritize ethical considerations.

Why It Matters:

- **Guidance:** Ethical guidelines provide clear principles to guide AI development.
- **Consistency:** Ensures that ethical considerations are consistently applied across AI projects.
- **Trust:** Promotes trust in AI systems by demonstrating a commitment to ethical standards.

Outcome: Organizations that adhere to ethical guidelines are better positioned to develop AI systems that are fair, transparent, and trustworthy.

Strategies for Ethical AI Development

To develop ethical AI systems, healthcare organizations should adopt best practices that prioritize transparency, accountability, and fairness.

Best Practices for Ethical AI Development:

1. **Transparency:** Ensure that AI algorithms are transparent and explainable. Provide clear documentation of how the algorithms work and the data they use.
2. **Accountability:** Establish accountability mechanisms to ensure that AI systems are used responsibly. This includes identifying individuals or teams responsible for overseeing AI deployments.
3. **Inclusiveness:** Involve diverse stakeholders in the AI development process to ensure that multiple perspectives are considered and that the system meets the needs of all users.
4. **Fairness:** Implement measures to identify and mitigate biases in AI systems. Ensure that the AI system performs equitably across different demographic groups.
5. **Continuous Evaluation:** Continuously evaluate the ethical implications of AI systems and make adjustments as needed to address emerging concerns.

Practical Do's and Don'ts for Ethical AI Implementation

Do's:

1. **Do Conduct Bias Audits:** Regularly audit AI systems for biases and take corrective actions to ensure fairness.
2. **Do Prioritize Data Privacy:** Implement robust data privacy and security measures to protect patient information.

3. **Do Promote Transparency:** Ensure that AI algorithms are transparent and explainable to build trust among users.
4. **Do Engage Diverse Stakeholders:** Involve a diverse group of stakeholders in the AI development process to ensure multiple perspectives are considered.
5. **Do Adhere to Ethical Guidelines:** Follow ethical guidelines and best practices to ensure that AI systems are developed and deployed responsibly.

Don'ts:

1. **Don't Ignore Bias:** Failing to address bias in AI systems can lead to unfair and harmful outcomes.
2. **Don't Skimp on Data Security:** Neglecting data security measures can result in data breaches and loss of patient trust.
3. **Don't Overlook Transparency:** Lack of transparency in AI algorithms can undermine trust and hinder adoption.
4. **Don't Exclude Stakeholders:** Excluding stakeholders from the AI development process can result in systems that do not meet user needs or ethical standards.
5. **Don't Ignore Continuous Evaluation:** Failing to continuously evaluate AI systems can lead to unchecked ethical concerns and reduced effectiveness.

Conclusion

Confronting the dark side of AI involves addressing bias, ensuring data privacy, and committing to ethical development practices. By implementing robust strategies for mitigating bias, protecting patient data, and adhering to ethical guidelines, healthcare organizations can develop AI systems that are fair, transparent, and trustworthy. Embracing these principles is essential for realizing the full potential of AI in healthcare and building systems that benefit all patients.

Bibliography

Mayo Clinic. (2019, September 10). "Mayo clinic selects Google as strategic partner for health care innovation, cloud computing [Press release]." https://newsnetwork.mayoclinic.org/discussion/mayo-clinic-selects-google-as-strategic-partner-for-health-care-innovation-cloud-computing/

Obermeyer, Z., Powers, B., Vogeli, C., & Mullainathan, S. (2019). "Dissecting racial bias in an algorithm used to manage the health of populations." Science, 366(6464), 447–453. https://doi.org/10.1126/science.aax2342 — https://www.science.org/doi/10.1126/science.aax2342

Ross, C., & Swetlitz, I. (2017, September 5). "IBM pitched its Watson supercomputer as a revolution in cancer care. It's nowhere close." STAT News. https://www.statnews.com/2017/09/05/watson-ibm-cancer/

World Health Organization. (2021). "Ethics and governance of artificial intelligence for health: WHO guidance." https://www.who.int/publications/i/item/9789240029200

Chapter 10

Impactful Metrics: Beyond Traditional KPIs

As Artificial Intelligence (AI) continues to integrate into healthcare, measuring its impact goes beyond traditional Key Performance Indicators (KPIs). While standard metrics such as cost savings and efficiency improvements are essential, they often fail to capture the full scope of AI's transformative potential. This chapter explores the need for new KPIs that accurately reflect AI's impact on healthcare, provides examples of these metrics, and offers practical guidance on implementing a comprehensive evaluation framework.

Challenging Traditional Metrics

Traditional KPIs in healthcare, such as patient throughput, readmission rates, and cost per patient, have long been the standard for measuring performance. However, these metrics may not fully capture the benefits and challenges of AI implementation.

DOI: 10.4324/9781003571407-14

The Limitations of Traditional KPIs

Traditional KPIs often focus on immediate, quantifiable outcomes. While these metrics are essential, they may overlook long-term benefits, qualitative improvements, and the broader implications of AI.

Example: Cost Savings vs. Patient Outcomes. A hospital might implement an AI-driven scheduling system that reduces operational costs by optimizing staff schedules. Traditional KPIs would measure the cost savings, but they might not capture the improvement in patient outcomes due to more efficient and less stressful working conditions for healthcare providers.

Why It Falls Short:

- **Short-Term Focus**: Traditional KPIs often emphasize immediate, short-term results.
- **Quantitative Bias**: They may overlook qualitative improvements, such as patient satisfaction and staff well-being.
- **Narrow Scope**: Focusing solely on financial metrics can miss the broader impact of AI on healthcare quality and accessibility.

Outcome: Relying solely on traditional KPIs can result in an incomplete understanding of AI's impact, potentially undervaluing its contributions.

New KPIs for AI in Healthcare

To fully capture the impact of AI, healthcare organizations need to develop new KPIs that reflect qualitative improvements, long-term benefits, and broader social implications.

Examples of New KPIs:

1. **Patient Satisfaction and Experience:** Measure improvements in patient satisfaction and experience, focusing on factors such as wait times, communication, and overall care quality.
2. **Clinical Accuracy and Diagnostic Improvement:** Evaluate the accuracy of AI-driven diagnostics and the improvement in clinical outcomes, such as earlier detection of diseases and more accurate diagnoses.
3. **Staff Satisfaction and Efficiency:** Assess the impact of AI on staff satisfaction and efficiency, including reductions in burnout and improvements in job satisfaction.
4. **Health Equity:** Measure the impact of AI on health equity, ensuring that AI systems provide fair and equitable care across different demographic groups.
5. **Innovation and Research Contributions:** Track the contributions of AI to medical research and innovation, such as the development of new treatments and the advancement of medical knowledge.
6. **Long-Term Health Outcomes:** Evaluate the long-term health outcomes of patients, such as reductions in chronic disease prevalence and improvements in population health.

Case Study: New KPIs in Action

Example: Cleveland Clinic's AI Implementation

Cleveland Clinic implemented an AI-driven system to improve patient triage in emergency departments. The traditional KPIs measured included cost savings and reduced wait times. However, Cleveland Clinic also developed new KPIs to capture the broader impact of the AI system.

New KPIs:

- **Patient Satisfaction:** Surveys showed a significant increase in patient satisfaction due to shorter wait times and more personalized care.
- **Clinical Accuracy:** The AI system improved the accuracy of initial diagnoses, leading to more appropriate and timely treatments.
- **Staff Efficiency and Morale:** Staff reported higher efficiency and job satisfaction, attributing it to the reduced stress and improved workflow.
- **Health Equity:** An audit revealed that the AI system provided equitable care across different patient demographics, with no significant disparities in outcomes.
- **Outcome:** By incorporating new KPIs, Cleveland Clinic gained a comprehensive understanding of the AI system's impact, demonstrating its value beyond traditional metrics.

Implementing a Comprehensive Evaluation Framework

To effectively measure the impact of AI, healthcare organizations should implement a comprehensive evaluation framework that includes both traditional and new KPIs.

Steps to Implement a Comprehensive Evaluation Framework:

1. **Define Objectives:** Clearly define the objectives of the AI implementation, aligning them with the organization's overall goals and mission.
2. **Identify Relevant KPIs:** Select a mix of traditional and new KPIs that accurately reflect the impact of the AI system on various aspects of healthcare delivery.
3. **Collect Baseline Data:** Gather baseline data for all selected KPIs before implementing the AI system to establish a point of comparison.

4. **Engage Stakeholders:** Involve a diverse group of stakeholders, including clinicians, patients, and administrators, in the KPI selection and evaluation process.
5. **Monitor and Analyze:** Continuously monitor the selected KPIs, analyzing the data to assess the AI system's performance and impact.
6. **Iterate and Improve:** Use the insights gained from KPI analysis to make iterative improvements to the AI system and the evaluation framework.
7. **Report and Communicate:** Regularly report the findings to all stakeholders, highlighting both successes and areas for improvement. Transparent communication fosters trust and collaboration.

Practical Do's and Don'ts for Measuring AI Impact

Do's:

1. **Do Include Qualitative and Quantitative KPIs:** Incorporate a mix of qualitative and quantitative KPIs to capture a comprehensive view of AI's impact.
2. **Do Focus on Long-Term Outcomes:** Measure long-term health outcomes and improvements to understand the sustained impact of AI.
3. **Do Engage Stakeholders:** Involve a diverse group of stakeholders in selecting and evaluating KPIs to ensure multiple perspectives are considered.
4. **Do Continuously Monitor and Adjust:** Regularly monitor KPIs and make adjustments to the AI system and evaluation framework based on the findings.
5. **Do Communicate Transparently:** Share the results of KPI evaluations openly with all stakeholders, fostering trust and collaboration.

Don'ts:

1. **Don't Rely Solely on Traditional KPIs:** Avoid focusing only on traditional metrics that may not capture the full scope of AI's impact.
2. **Don't Overlook Qualitative Improvements:** Ensure that qualitative improvements, such as patient and staff satisfaction, are included in the evaluation.
3. **Don't Ignore Health Equity:** Measure and address any disparities in care to ensure that AI systems provide equitable outcomes for all patient groups.
4. **Don't Neglect Continuous Improvement:** Use KPI evaluations to identify areas for improvement and make iterative changes to the AI system.
5. **Don't Underestimate the Importance of Baseline Data:** Collect baseline data before AI implementation to provide a clear point of comparison for evaluating impact.

Conclusion

Measuring the impact of AI in healthcare requires moving beyond traditional KPIs to include new metrics that capture qualitative improvements, long-term benefits, and broader social implications. By implementing a comprehensive evaluation framework and following best practices for measuring AI impact, healthcare organizations can gain a deeper understanding of AI's contributions and make data-driven decisions to enhance patient care and operational efficiency. The future of AI in healthcare is bright, and with the right metrics, organizations can fully realize its transformative potential.

Bibliography

Levin, S., et al. (2018). "Machine-learning-based electronic triage more accurately differentiates patients with respect to clinical outcomes compared with the emergency severity index." Annals of Emergency Medicine, 71(5), 565–574. https://doi.org/10.1016/j.annemergmed.2017.08.005

Obermeyer, Z., Powers, B., Vogeli, C., & Mullainathan, S. (2019). "Dissecting racial bias in an algorithm used to manage the health of populations." Science, 366(6464), 447–453. https://doi.org/10.1126/science.aax2342

Ross, C., & Swetlitz, I. (2017, September 5). "IBM pitched its Watson supercomputer as a revolution in cancer care. It's nowhere close." STAT News. https://www.statnews.com/2017/09/05/watson-ibm-cancer/

World Health Organization. (2021). "Ethics and governance of artificial intelligence for health: WHO guidance." https://www.who.int/publications/i/item/9789240029200

Chapter 11

Trench Stories: Real-World AI Case Studies

Theoretical knowledge and strategic frameworks are invaluable, but there's no substitute for real-world experience. In this chapter, we dive into the trenches of AI implementation in healthcare, sharing unfiltered stories of AI successes and failures. These case studies offer insider insights and hard-earned lessons, providing a candid look at what works, what doesn't, and why.

Unfiltered Stories of AI Successes

Case Study: AI-Powered Stroke Detection at Mount Sinai Health System

Background: Mount Sinai Health System in New York implemented an AI-driven tool for the early detection of strokes. The AI system, developed by Viz.ai, analyzes CT scans to identify signs of stroke and alert neurologists in real time.

DOI: 10.4324/9781003571407-15

Implementation: The AI tool was integrated into the hospital's existing workflow, ensuring that radiologists and neurologists could quickly access and act on AI-generated insights.

Outcomes:

- **Speed:** The AI system reduced the time from scan to treatment decision by 90 minutes on average.
- **Accuracy:** It improved the accuracy of stroke detection, leading to better patient outcomes.
- **Efficiency:** The system streamlined the workflow, allowing healthcare providers to focus on patient care rather than administrative tasks.

Key Takeaway: Integrating AI tools into existing workflows and ensuring real-time access to AI-generated insights can significantly improve clinical outcomes and operational efficiency.

Case Study: Personalized Diabetes Management at Joslin Diabetes Center

Background: Joslin Diabetes Center, a global leader in diabetes care, implemented an AI-driven platform to personalize diabetes management for its patients. The platform uses machine learning algorithms to analyze patient data and provide tailored treatment recommendations.

Implementation: The AI system was integrated with electronic health records (EHRs) to gather comprehensive patient data. It provided personalized insights and recommendations to both patients and healthcare providers.

Outcomes:

- **Personalization:** The AI platform enabled personalized treatment plans, improving patient adherence to medication and lifestyle recommendations.

- **Engagement:** Patients reported higher engagement with their treatment plans due to the tailored advice.
- **Clinical Outcomes:** There was a significant reduction in HbA1c levels among patients using the AI-driven platform.

Key Takeaway: Personalized AI-driven treatment plans can enhance patient engagement and improve clinical outcomes, particularly in chronic disease management.

Unfiltered Stories of AI Failures

Case Study: IBM Watson for Oncology at MD Anderson Cancer Center

Background: MD Anderson Cancer Center partnered with IBM Watson to develop an AI system for oncology. The goal was to use AI to assist oncologists in developing personalized cancer treatment plans.

Implementation: The AI system was trained on vast amounts of medical literature and patient data to generate treatment recommendations.

Outcomes:

- **Inconsistencies:** The AI system provided treatment recommendations that were often inconsistent with those of experienced oncologists.
- **Integration Issues:** There were significant challenges in integrating the AI system with MD Anderson's existing IT infrastructure.
- **Cost Overruns:** The project faced substantial cost overruns, leading to its eventual suspension.

Key Takeaway: Successful AI implementation requires careful integration with existing systems, consistent performance, and realistic expectations regarding costs and outcomes.

Case Study: Google Health's AI for Retinal Disease Detection in Thailand

Background: Google Health developed an AI system to detect retinal diseases in diabetic patients, aiming to improve early detection and treatment in rural Thailand.

Implementation: The AI system was deployed in local clinics to analyze retinal images and provide diagnostic insights.

Outcomes:

- **Operational Challenges:** The system struggled with varying image quality due to differences in camera equipment and operator skills.
- **Contextual Limitations:** The AI system failed to account for local clinical practices and infrastructure limitations, leading to workflow disruptions.
- **Adoption Barriers:** There was resistance from local healthcare providers who were unfamiliar with the technology and skeptical of its recommendations.

Key Takeaway: AI implementations must consider local contexts, including equipment variability, clinical practices, and stakeholder readiness, to be successful.

Insider Insights and Hard-Earned Lessons

Lesson 1: Start Small and Scale

Many successful AI implementations start with small, focused pilot projects. This approach allows organizations to test the technology, gather feedback, and make necessary adjustments before scaling up.

Example: The Mayo Clinic's iterative approach to AI-driven predictive analytics began with a small pilot project focused on predicting patient readmissions. The success of the pilot provided a blueprint for scaling the AI system across the organization.

Lesson 2: Engage End-Users Early

Involving end-users – such as clinicians, nurses, and administrative staff – in the development and implementation process is crucial for ensuring the AI system meets their needs and fits seamlessly into existing workflows.

Example: Mount Sinai Health System's successful implementation of AI-powered stroke detection involved extensive collaboration with radiologists and neurologists, ensuring the tool complemented their workflows and provided actionable insights.

Lesson 3: Prioritize Data Quality

High-quality data is the foundation of effective AI systems. Ensuring that data used for training AI models is accurate, diverse, and representative of the patient population is critical.

Example: Joslin Diabetes Center's personalized diabetes management platform leveraged comprehensive and high-quality patient data from EHRs to provide accurate and tailored treatment recommendations.

Lesson 4: Address Ethical and Regulatory Considerations

Ethical and regulatory considerations, such as patient privacy, data security, and bias, must be addressed proactively to build trust and ensure compliance.

Example: Google Health's AI for retinal disease detection faced ethical and operational challenges due to varying image quality and local clinical practices. Addressing these considerations early on could have mitigated some of the implementation issues.

Practical Do's and Don'ts for AI Implementation

Do's:

1. **Do Start with Pilot Projects:** Test AI systems on a small scale to gather feedback and make adjustments before full-scale implementation.
2. **Do Engage End-Users:** Involve clinicians, nurses, and administrative staff early in the development process to ensure the AI system meets their needs.
3. **Do Prioritize Data Quality:** Invest in high-quality data collection and cleaning processes to ensure accurate and reliable AI predictions.
4. **Do Address Ethical and Regulatory Considerations:** Proactively address issues such as patient privacy, data security, and bias to build trust and ensure compliance.
5. **Do Provide Comprehensive Training:** Offer thorough training to all users to ensure they understand how to effectively use the AI system.

Don'ts:

1. **Don't Expect Perfection from the Start:** AI systems often require refinement and improvement. Don't expect them to be perfect from the beginning.
2. **Don't Neglect Integration:** Ensure the AI system integrates seamlessly with existing IT infrastructure and workflows to avoid disruptions.

3. **Don't Overlook Local Context:** Consider local clinical practices, equipment variability, and stakeholder readiness when implementing AI systems in diverse settings.
4. **Don't Underestimate Costs:** Be realistic about the costs associated with AI implementation, including integration, training, and ongoing maintenance.
5. **Don't Ignore Continuous Monitoring:** Regularly monitor AI systems to identify and address issues, gather feedback, and make iterative improvements.

Conclusion

Real-world case studies of AI implementation in healthcare provide invaluable insights into what works, what doesn't, and why. By learning from these successes and failures, healthcare organizations can navigate the complexities of AI adoption and harness its full potential. Starting small, engaging end-users, prioritizing data quality, and addressing ethical considerations are key strategies for successful AI implementation. With these lessons in mind, healthcare organizations can drive meaningful improvements in patient care and operational efficiency.

Bibliography

Bora, A., et al. (2021). Predicting the risk of developing diabetic retinopathy using deep learning. *The Lancet Digital Health*, 3(1), e10–e19. https://doi.org/10.1016/S2589-7500(20)30250-8 (Joslin Diabetes Center collaborated on dataset and validation.)

Gulshan, V., Peng, L., Coram, M., Stumpe, M. C., Wu, D., Narayanaswamy, A., Venugopalan, S., Widner, K., Madams, T., Cuadros, J., Kim, R., Raman, R., Nelson, P. C., Mega, J. L., & Webster, D. R. (2016). "Development and validation of a deep learning algorithm for detection of diabetic retinopathy in retinal fundus photographs." JAMA, 316(22), 2402–2410. https://doi.org/10.1001/jama.2016.17216 — Google Research overview: https://research.google/blog/deep-learning-for-detection-of-diabetic-eye-disease/

Herper, M. (2017, February 19). MD Anderson benches IBM Watson in setback for artificial intelligence in medicine. Forbes. — peer-reviewed coverage: Schmidt, C. (2017). M.D. Anderson breaks with IBM Watson, raising questions about artificial intelligence in oncology. *Journal of the National Cancer Institute*, 109(5), djx113. https://doi.org/10.1093/jnci/djx113

Mayo Clinic Platform. (n.d.). Mayo Clinic Platform — Transforming healthcare through data and AI. — primary announcement: Mayo Clinic. (2019, September 10). *Mayo Clinic selects Google as strategic partner for health care innovation, cloud computing.* https://newsnetwork.mayoclinic.org/discussion/mayo-clinic-selects-google-as-strategic-partner-for-health-care-innovation-cloud-computing/

Morey, J. R., Fiano, E., Yaeger, K. A., Zhang, X., & Fifi, J. T. (2021). "Impact of Viz LVO on time-to-treatment and clinical outcomes in large vessel occlusion stroke patients presenting to primary stroke centers." Frontiers in Neurology, 12, 651610. https://doi.org/10.3389/fneur.2021.651610 (Mount Sinai Health System real-world implementation of Viz.ai LVO stroke detection.)

Obermeyer, Z., Powers, B., Vogeli, C., & Mullainathan, S. (2019). "Dissecting racial bias in an algorithm used to manage the health of populations." Science, 366(6464), 447–453. https://doi.org/10.1126/science.aax2342

Silva, P. S., Cavallerano, J. D., Haddad, N. M. N., Kwak, H., Dyer, K. H., Omar, A. F., Shikari, H., Aiello, L. M., Sun, J. K., & Aiello, L. P. (2015). Peripheral lesions identified on ultrawide field imaging predict increased risk of diabetic retinopathy progression over 4 years. *Ophthalmology*, 122(5), 949–956. **DOI:** https://doi.org/10.1016/j.ophtha.2015.01.008 **PubMed ID:** 25704318 **PubMed URL:** https://pubmed.ncbi.nlm.nih.gov/25704318/

Stanford Center for Artificial Intelligence in Medicine and Imaging (AIMI). (n.d.). Stanford AIMI. https://aimi.stanford.edu/

Chapter 12

AI's Uncertain Future: Preparing for the Unpredictable

Artificial Intelligence (AI) is already transforming healthcare, but its future is anything but certain. As AI technologies continue to evolve at a rapid pace, healthcare organizations must prepare for the unpredictable. This chapter explores the potential future advancements in AI, the challenges and opportunities they present, and strategies for future-proofing AI strategies. We'll speculate on controversial and disruptive trends, providing insights into how healthcare can stay ahead of the curve.

The Unpredictability of AI Advancements

AI is a dynamic and rapidly advancing field, with new breakthroughs occurring regularly. This unpredictability makes it challenging for healthcare organizations to plan long-term

DOI: 10.4324/9781003571407-16

AI strategies. However, understanding the potential future directions of AI can help organizations prepare for upcoming changes.

Potential Future Advancements in AI:

1. **Explainable AI (XAI):** As AI systems become more complex, the need for transparency and explainability increases. XAI aims to make AI decisions more understandable to humans, fostering trust and enabling better decision-making.
2. **AI-Augmented Healthcare Professionals:** AI is expected to augment the capabilities of healthcare professionals rather than replace them. Future AI systems could provide real-time assistance, offering insights and recommendations to support clinical decision-making.
3. **Personalized Medicine:** AI will likely play a critical role in advancing personalized medicine, enabling tailored treatments based on individual genetic, environmental, and lifestyle factors.
4. **Integration of AI with IoT:** The Internet of Things (IoT) will increasingly integrate with AI, allowing for continuous monitoring and real-time analysis of patient data from wearable devices and smart home technologies.
5. **AI in Preventive Healthcare:** AI's predictive capabilities will be leveraged for preventive healthcare, identifying risk factors and early warning signs to prevent diseases before they develop.

Challenges and Opportunities

While these advancements offer significant opportunities, they also present challenges that healthcare organizations must navigate.

Challenges:

- **Data Privacy and Security:** Ensuring patient data privacy and security becomes more complex as AI systems become more integrated and pervasive.
- **Bias and Fairness:** Mitigating bias in AI systems remains a critical concern, requiring ongoing vigilance and intervention.
- **Regulatory Compliance:** Keeping up with evolving regulations and ensuring compliance is a continuous challenge.
- **Ethical Considerations:** Addressing the ethical implications of AI, such as decision-making transparency and accountability, is essential for maintaining trust.

Opportunities:

- **Improved Patient Outcomes:** AI has the potential to significantly improve patient outcomes through more accurate diagnoses, personalized treatments, and preventive care.
- **Operational Efficiency:** AI can streamline healthcare operations, reducing costs and improving efficiency.
- **Enhanced Research and Innovation:** AI will accelerate medical research and innovation, leading to new treatments and therapies.
- **Patient Engagement:** AI-powered tools can enhance patient engagement, providing personalized health information and support.

Future-Proofing AI Strategies

To prepare for the unpredictable future of AI, healthcare organizations must adopt strategies that are flexible, adaptive, and forward-thinking.

Strategies for Future-Proofing AI:

1. **Adopt a Flexible AI Strategy:** Develop an AI strategy that is flexible and adaptable to changing technologies and market conditions. This includes being open to new AI applications and willing to pivot when necessary.
2. **Invest in Continuous Learning:** Stay updated with the latest AI advancements by investing in continuous learning and professional development for staff. Encourage participation in AI conferences, workshops, and training programs.
3. **Build a Robust Data Infrastructure:** Ensure that your organization's data infrastructure is capable of supporting advanced AI applications. This includes investing in high-quality data collection, storage, and processing capabilities.
4. **Foster a Culture of Innovation:** Create an organizational culture that encourages experimentation and innovation. Provide opportunities for staff to explore new AI technologies and develop innovative solutions.
5. **Collaborate with AI Experts and Partners:** Collaborate with AI experts, research institutions, and technology partners to stay at the forefront of AI advancements. These partnerships can provide access to cutting-edge technologies and expertise.
6. **Focus on Ethical AI Development:** Prioritize ethical considerations in AI development and implementation. Establish ethical guidelines and frameworks to ensure that AI systems are transparent, fair, and accountable.

Speculating on Controversial and Disruptive Trends

The future of AI in healthcare is likely to include controversial and disruptive trends that will challenge the status quo. Here are some speculative trends that could shape the future of AI in healthcare.

AI-Driven Autonomous Healthcare

Speculation: AI-driven autonomous healthcare systems, such as AI-powered robotic surgeons and autonomous diagnostic tools, could become a reality. These systems would operate with minimal human intervention, potentially transforming healthcare delivery.

Opportunities:

- **Increased Access:** Autonomous systems could provide healthcare services in underserved areas with limited access to human healthcare professionals.
- **Efficiency:** Autonomous systems could operate 24/7, providing continuous care and reducing wait times.

Challenges:

- **Ethical Concerns:** The ethical implications of autonomous healthcare, such as accountability for errors and patient trust, must be carefully considered.
- **Regulatory Hurdles:** Ensuring that autonomous systems meet stringent regulatory standards will be a significant challenge.

AI and Genetic Editing

Speculation: AI could accelerate advancements in genetic editing technologies, such as CRISPR, enabling precise modifications to human DNA to treat genetic disorders and enhance human capabilities.

Opportunities:

- **Cure Genetic Disorders:** AI-enhanced genetic editing could lead to cures for genetic disorders that are currently untreatable.
- **Personalized Enhancements:** Genetic editing could be tailored to individual needs, enhancing physical and cognitive abilities.

Challenges:

- **Ethical Dilemmas:** The ethical implications of genetic editing, such as the potential for "designer babies" and genetic inequality, must be addressed.
- **Social Acceptance:** Gaining public acceptance for genetic editing technologies will require careful communication and ethical considerations.

AI-Enhanced Human-Machine Interfaces

Speculation: AI-enhanced human-machine interfaces, such as brain-computer interfaces (BCIs), could enable direct communication between the human brain and external devices, transforming how we interact with technology.

Opportunities:

- **Enhanced Mobility:** BCIs could restore mobility for individuals with paralysis by enabling control of prosthetic limbs and exoskeletons.
- **Cognitive Enhancement:** BCIs could enhance cognitive functions, such as memory and learning, by directly interfacing with the brain.

Challenges:

- **Privacy Concerns:** The direct interface with the brain raises significant privacy concerns, including the potential for unauthorized access to thoughts and memories.
- **Technical and Ethical Hurdles:** Developing safe and effective BCIs will require overcoming significant technical and ethical challenges.

Conclusion

The future of AI in healthcare is both exciting and uncertain. By anticipating potential advancements, challenges, and opportunities, healthcare organizations can prepare for the unpredictable and leverage AI to drive meaningful improvements in patient care and operational efficiency. Adopting flexible strategies, investing in continuous learning, building robust data infrastructures, fostering a culture of innovation, and focusing on ethical AI development are key to future-proofing AI strategies. As we navigate the rapidly evolving landscape of AI, staying adaptable and forward-thinking will be crucial for success.

Bibliography

Bora, A., Balasubramanian, S., Babenko, B., Virmani, S., Venugopalan, S., Mitani, A., de Oliveira Marinho, G., Cuadros, J., Ruamviboonsuk, P., Corrado, G. S., Peng, L., Webster, D. R., Varadarajan, A. V., Hammel, N., Liu, Y., & Bavishi, P. (2021). “Predicting the risk of developing diabetic retinopathy using deep learning.” The Lancet Digital Health, 3(1), e10–e19. https://doi.org/10.1016/S2589-7500(20)30250-8 (validated on Joslin Diabetes Center data)

Gulshan, V., Peng, L., Coram, M., Stumpe, M. C., Wu, D., Narayanaswamy, A., Venugopalan, S., Widner, K., Madams, T., Cuadros, J., Kim, R., Raman, R., Nelson, P. C., Mega, J. L., & Webster, D. R. (2016). “Development and validation of a deep learning algorithm for detection of diabetic retinopathy in retinal fundus photographs.” JAMA, 316(22), 2402–2410. https://doi.org/10.1001/jama.2016.17216 — Google Research overview: https://research.google/blog/deep-learning-for-detection-of-diabetic-eye-disease/

Mayo Clinic. (2019, September 10). “Mayo Clinic selects Google as strategic partner for health care innovation, cloud computing [Press release].” https://newsnetwork.mayoclinic.org/discussion/mayo-clinic-selects-google-as-strategic-partner-for-health-care-innovation-cloud-computing/ — program page: https://www.mayoclinicplatform.org/

Obermeyer, Z., Powers, B., Vogeli, C., & Mullainathan, S. (2019). “Dissecting racial bias in an algorithm used to manage the health of populations.” Science, 366(6464), 447–453. https://doi.org/10.1126/science.aax2342

Schmidt, C. (2017). "M.D. Anderson breaks with IBM Watson, raising questions about artificial intelligence in oncology." Journal of the National Cancer Institute, 109(5), djx113. https://doi.org/10.1093/jnci/djx113 — see also: Herper, M. (2017, February 19). MD Anderson benches IBM Watson in setback for artificial intelligence in medicine. Forbes. https://www.forbes.com/sites/matthewherper/2017/02/19/md-anderson-benches-ibm-watson-in-setback-for-artificial-intelligence-in-medicine/

World Health Organization. (2021). "Ethics and governance of artificial intelligence for health: WHO guidance." https://www.who.int/publications/i/item/9789240029200

THE FUTURE OF AI IN HEALTHCARE

IV

Chapter 13

The Next Frontier in AI Diagnostics and Treatment

Artificial Intelligence (AI) is on the cusp of revolutionizing diagnostics and treatment in healthcare. With advancements in machine learning, deep learning, and other AI technologies, healthcare professionals are gaining new tools to diagnose diseases earlier, personalize treatments, and improve patient outcomes. This chapter explores the latest innovations in AI diagnostics and treatment, highlighting real-world examples, discussing potential challenges, and offering insights into the future of AI in healthcare.

Personalized Medicine and Predictive Analytics

Personalized medicine tailors treatments to individual patients based on their genetic, environmental, and lifestyle factors. AI plays a crucial role in advancing personalized medicine by

DOI: 10.4324/9781003571407-18

analyzing vast amounts of data to identify patterns and make accurate predictions.

Use Case: AI-Driven Personalized Treatment Plans

Example: Tempus. Tempus, a technology company, uses AI to analyze clinical and molecular data to provide personalized treatment recommendations for cancer patients. By integrating genomic sequencing data with clinical information, Tempus's AI platform identifies the most effective treatment options for individual patients.

Outcomes:

- **Improved Outcomes:** Patients receive treatments tailored to their genetic profiles, leading to better clinical outcomes.
- **Reduced Trial and Error:** AI reduces the trial-and-error approach in cancer treatment, saving time and reducing side effects.
- **Enhanced Research:** The data collected and analyzed by Tempus contributes to ongoing cancer research and the development of new therapies.

Key Takeaway: AI-driven personalized treatment plans can significantly improve patient outcomes by tailoring treatments to individual needs and genetic profiles.

Future Technologies and Innovations

The future of AI in diagnostics and treatment is promising, with several emerging technologies poised to transform healthcare.

AI in Radiology: Advanced Imaging Techniques

AI is revolutionizing radiology by improving the accuracy and efficiency of medical imaging. Advanced AI algorithms can detect abnormalities in medical images that may be missed by human radiologists.

Example: Aidoc. Aidoc is an AI-powered radiology platform that uses deep learning to analyze medical images and detect critical findings, such as intracranial hemorrhages and pulmonary embolisms. The platform prioritizes cases based on urgency, enabling radiologists to focus on the most critical patients first.

Outcomes:

- **Increased Accuracy:** Aidoc's AI algorithms have demonstrated higher accuracy in detecting abnormalities compared to traditional methods.
- **Reduced Workload:** The platform reduces the workload for radiologists by prioritizing urgent cases and automating the detection process.
- **Faster Diagnosis:** Patients receive faster diagnoses, leading to quicker treatment and better outcomes.

Key Takeaway: AI in radiology enhances the accuracy and efficiency of medical imaging, improving diagnostic capabilities and patient outcomes.

AI in Pathology: Digitizing Tissue Analysis

AI is also making significant strides in pathology, where it is used to analyze tissue samples and identify diseases at a cellular level.

Example: PathAI. PathAI is an AI-powered platform that uses machine learning to analyze pathology slides and provide accurate diagnoses. The platform can detect cancerous cells, classify tumor types, and assess disease severity with high precision.

Outcomes:

- **Enhanced Accuracy:** PathAI's algorithms provide highly accurate diagnoses, reducing the risk of human error.
- **Consistency:** The platform ensures consistent diagnostic standards across different pathologists and institutions.
- **Time Efficiency:** AI accelerates the diagnostic process, allowing for faster treatment decisions.

Key Takeaway: AI in pathology offers highly accurate and consistent diagnostic capabilities, transforming tissue analysis and disease detection.

Potential Challenges and Considerations

While the potential of AI in diagnostics and treatment is immense, several challenges must be addressed to ensure successful implementation.

Data Quality and Privacy

High-quality data is essential for training accurate AI models. However, ensuring data privacy and security is equally important.

Challenges:

- **Data Quality:** AI models require large amounts of high-quality, annotated data. Inconsistent or incomplete data can lead to inaccurate predictions.

- **Privacy Concerns:** Protecting patient data and ensuring compliance with regulations like HIPAA is crucial.

Solutions:

- **Data Curation:** Invest in data curation and annotation processes to ensure high-quality data.
- **Privacy Measures:** Implement robust data encryption, access controls, and anonymization techniques to protect patient data.

Integration with Clinical Workflows

Integrating AI systems into existing clinical workflows can be challenging, especially if the technology disrupts established processes.

Challenges:

- **Workflow Disruption:** AI systems may require changes to clinical workflows, leading to resistance from healthcare providers.
- **Training Needs:** Clinicians need training to effectively use AI tools and interpret their outputs.

Solutions:

- **User-Friendly Design:** Develop AI tools with intuitive interfaces that integrate seamlessly into existing workflows.
- **Comprehensive Training:** Provide comprehensive training programs to ensure clinicians are comfortable using AI tools.

Ethical and Regulatory Considerations

The use of AI in healthcare raises ethical and regulatory questions, including issues of bias, transparency, and accountability.

Challenges:

- **Bias and Fairness:** AI models can inherit biases from training data, leading to unequal treatment outcomes.
- **Transparency:** Ensuring AI decision-making processes are transparent and explainable is essential for trust.
- **Regulatory Compliance:** Navigating the regulatory landscape for AI in healthcare can be complex.

Solutions:

- **Bias Mitigation:** Implement strategies to identify and mitigate biases in AI models.
- **Explainable AI:** Develop AI systems that provide clear explanations for their decisions.
- **Regulatory Guidance:** Work closely with regulatory bodies to ensure compliance and stay updated with evolving regulations.

The Future of AI in Diagnostics and Treatment

The future of AI in diagnostics and treatment holds tremendous potential, with several trends likely to shape the landscape.

AI and Genomic Medicine

AI is expected to play a crucial role in advancing genomic medicine by analyzing genetic data to identify disease predispositions and guide personalized treatments.

Example: Deep Genomics. Deep Genomics uses AI to analyze genetic data and predict the impact of genetic variations on diseases. The platform helps identify potential therapeutic targets and develop personalized treatments.

Outcomes:

- **Precision Medicine:** AI-driven genomic analysis enables highly personalized treatments based on an individual's genetic makeup.
- **Early Detection:** Identifying genetic predispositions allows for early intervention and preventive measures.

Key Takeaway: AI in genomic medicine paves the way for precision medicine, offering personalized treatments and early disease detection.

AI and Remote Monitoring

The integration of AI with remote monitoring technologies, such as wearable devices and smart home systems, will enable continuous health monitoring and early detection of health issues.

Example: Apple Health. Apple Health uses AI to analyze data from wearable devices, such as the Apple Watch, to monitor heart health and detect abnormalities like atrial fibrillation.

Outcomes:

- **Continuous Monitoring:** AI enables continuous health monitoring, providing real-time insights into a patient's health status.
- **Early Intervention:** Early detection of health issues allows for timely intervention and improved outcomes.

Key Takeaway: AI-powered remote monitoring offers continuous health insights, enabling early detection and intervention for better health management.

Practical Do's and Don'ts for Implementing AI in Diagnostics and Treatment

Do's:

- **Do Ensure Data Quality:** Invest in high-quality data collection and annotation processes to train accurate AI models.
- **Do Focus on Integration:** Develop AI tools that integrate seamlessly with existing clinical workflows and provide intuitive user interfaces.
- **Do Provide Comprehensive Training:** Offer thorough training programs for clinicians to ensure they are comfortable using AI tools and interpreting their outputs.
- **Do Address Ethical Considerations:** Implement strategies to mitigate bias, ensure transparency, and maintain regulatory compliance.
- **Do Foster Collaboration:** Collaborate with AI experts, healthcare professionals, and regulatory bodies to develop and implement AI systems effectively.

Don'ts:

- **Don't Overlook Privacy:** Ensure robust data privacy and security measures to protect patient information.
- **Don't Ignore User Feedback:** Continuously gather and incorporate feedback from healthcare providers to improve AI tools and their usability.
- **Don't Neglect Explainability:** Develop AI systems that provide clear and understandable explanations for their decisions to build trust among users.
- **Don't Underestimate Integration Challenges:** Consider potential workflow disruptions and plan for smooth integration of AI tools into clinical practice.
- **Don't Forget Long-Term Monitoring:** Continuously monitor the performance of AI systems and make iterative improvements based on real-world data and feedback.

Conclusion

The next frontier in AI diagnostics and treatment promises to transform healthcare by enabling personalized medicine, improving diagnostic accuracy, and enhancing treatment outcomes. By embracing emerging technologies, addressing potential challenges, and implementing best practices, healthcare organizations can harness the power of AI to drive innovation and improve patient care. The future of AI in healthcare is bright, and with careful planning and execution, its potential can be fully realized.

Bibliography

Aidoc. (n.d.). "Radiology AI imaging — Faster, smarter care." https://www.aidoc.com/solutions/radiology/

Deep Genomics, Inc. (n.d.). "Deep genomics — AI platform for genomic medicine." https://www.deepgenomics.com/AI-Platform/

Obermeyer, Z., Powers, B., Vogeli, C., & Mullainathan, S. (2019). "Dissecting racial bias in an algorithm used to manage the health of populations." Science, 366(6464), 447–453. https://doi.org/10.1126/science.aax2342

PathAI, Inc. (n.d.). "PathAI — Pathology transformed." https://www.pathai.com/

Perez, M. V., Mahaffey, K. W., Hedlin, H., Rumsfeld, J. S., Garcia, A., Ferris, T., Balasubramanian, V., Russo, A. M., Rajmane, A., Cheung, L., Hung, G., Lee, J., Kowey, P., Talati, N., Nag, D., Gummidipundi, S. E., Beatty, A., Hills, M. T., Desai, S., … Turakhia, M. P. (2019). "Large-scale assessment of a smartwatch to identify atrial fibrillation." New England Journal of Medicine, 381(20), 1909–1917. — Apple technical overview: https://www.apple.com/healthcare/docs/site/Apple_Watch_Arrhythmia_Detection.pdf

Tempus AI, Inc. (n.d.). "Tempus — AI-powered precision medicine and genomic testing." https://www.tempus.com/

Chapter 14

AI and Telehealth: Expanding Access to Care

The convergence of Artificial Intelligence (AI) and telehealth is reshaping the landscape of healthcare delivery. By leveraging AI technologies, telehealth platforms can provide more accurate diagnoses, personalized treatment plans, and improved patient engagement, all while expanding access to care for underserved populations. This chapter explores the synergies between AI and telehealth, real-world use cases, the challenges and opportunities they present, and practical guidance for integrating AI with telehealth platforms.

The Rise of Telehealth

Telehealth has seen exponential growth, particularly accelerated by the COVID-19 pandemic. The ability to deliver healthcare services remotely has proven invaluable in

DOI: 10.4324/9781003571407-19

maintaining continuity of care while minimizing the risk of virus transmission.

Benefits of Telehealth

1. **Accessibility:** Telehealth breaks down geographical barriers, providing access to healthcare for patients in remote or underserved areas.
2. **Convenience:** Patients can receive medical consultations from the comfort of their homes, reducing the need for travel and wait times.
3. **Continuity of Care:** Telehealth facilitates continuous monitoring and follow-up, essential for managing chronic conditions and post-operative care.
4. **Cost-Effectiveness:** Reducing the need for in-person visits can lower healthcare costs for both providers and patients.

Integrating AI with Telehealth Platforms

The integration of AI with telehealth platforms enhances their capabilities, making remote healthcare delivery more efficient, accurate, and personalized.

Use Case: AI-Powered Virtual Assistants

Example: Babylon Health. Babylon Health uses AI-powered virtual assistants to conduct initial patient assessments through telehealth platforms. These virtual assistants use natural language processing (NLP) to understand patient symptoms and medical history, providing preliminary diagnoses and recommendations.

Outcomes:

- **Efficiency:** AI virtual assistants handle routine inquiries and assessments, freeing up healthcare professionals for more complex cases.
- **Accuracy:** The AI system provides accurate preliminary diagnoses, improving the quality of care.
- **Patient Engagement:** Patients receive immediate responses and guidance, enhancing their engagement and satisfaction.

Key Takeaway: AI-powered virtual assistants streamline the telehealth process, improving efficiency and patient experience.

Use Case: Remote Monitoring and Predictive Analytics

Example: Livongo. Livongo, a chronic disease management company, integrates AI with telehealth to provide personalized health insights and recommendations. The platform uses AI to analyze data from remote monitoring devices, such as glucometers and blood pressure monitors, and predict potential health issues.

Outcomes:

- **Proactive Care:** Predictive analytics enable early intervention, preventing complications and hospitalizations.
- **Personalization:** Patients receive tailored recommendations based on their health data, improving adherence to treatment plans.
- **Continuous Monitoring:** AI-driven remote monitoring provides real-time insights into patient health, allowing for timely adjustments to care plans.

Key Takeaway: AI integration with remote monitoring enhances chronic disease management by enabling proactive and personalized care.

Use Case: Telepsychiatry and AI

Example: Woebot Health. Woebot Health offers an AI-powered mental health chatbot that provides cognitive behavioral therapy (CBT) through telehealth platforms. The chatbot uses NLP to interact with patients, offering support and therapeutic techniques.

Outcomes:

- **Accessibility:** AI-driven telepsychiatry expands access to mental health support, particularly in areas with limited mental health services.
- **Engagement:** Patients can engage with the chatbot anytime, reducing barriers to seeking help.
- **Consistency:** The AI provides consistent therapeutic support, complementing human therapists.

Key Takeaway: AI-powered telepsychiatry enhances access to mental health support and provides consistent, on-demand care.

Challenges and Opportunities

While the integration of AI and telehealth offers significant benefits, it also presents challenges that must be addressed to ensure successful implementation.

Challenges:

1. **Data Privacy and Security:** Ensuring the privacy and security of patient data is paramount, especially when integrating AI with telehealth platforms that handle sensitive health information.
2. **Technical Integration:** Seamlessly integrating AI technologies with existing telehealth infrastructure can be complex and requires robust technical expertise.

3. **Regulatory Compliance:** Navigating the regulatory landscape for AI and telehealth is challenging, with varying requirements across different regions.
4. **Digital Divide:** Access to telehealth and AI technologies may be limited for certain populations due to disparities in digital literacy and internet connectivity.

Opportunities:

1. **Enhanced Access to Care:** AI and telehealth can bridge the gap in healthcare access, particularly for underserved and remote populations.
2. **Improved Quality of Care:** AI-enhanced telehealth platforms can provide more accurate diagnoses, personalized treatment plans, and continuous monitoring, improving overall care quality.
3. **Cost Savings:** Reducing the need for in-person visits and hospitalizations can lower healthcare costs for providers and patients.
4. **Patient Empowerment:** AI-driven telehealth tools empower patients to take an active role in managing their health, leading to better outcomes and satisfaction.

Practical Do's and Don'ts for Integrating AI with Telehealth

Do's:

1. **Do Prioritize Data Security:** Implement robust data security measures to protect patient information and ensure compliance with privacy regulations.
2. **Do Ensure Seamless Integration:** Develop AI solutions that integrate seamlessly with existing telehealth platforms to avoid disruptions in care delivery.
3. **Do Provide Comprehensive Training:** Offer training programs for healthcare providers and patients to ensure they can effectively use AI-enhanced telehealth tools.

4. **Do Focus on User Experience:** Design AI-driven telehealth tools with a user-friendly interface to enhance patient engagement and satisfaction.
5. **Do Address the Digital Divide:** Implement strategies to improve access to telehealth and AI technologies for populations with limited digital literacy and connectivity.

Don'ts:

1. **Don't Overlook Ethical Considerations:** Address ethical concerns, such as bias in AI algorithms and equitable access to care, to build trust and ensure fairness.
2. **Don't Neglect Continuous Monitoring:** Regularly monitor AI-driven telehealth systems to identify issues, gather feedback, and make iterative improvements.
3. **Don't Ignore Regulatory Requirements:** Stay informed about regulatory requirements and ensure compliance to avoid legal and financial repercussions.
4. **Don't Underestimate Integration Challenges:** Plan for technical integration challenges and allocate resources to address them effectively.
5. **Don't Forget Patient Education:** Educate patients about the benefits and limitations of AI-enhanced telehealth to set realistic expectations and build trust.

Conclusion

The integration of AI with telehealth is expanding access to care, improving the quality of healthcare delivery, and empowering patients. By addressing challenges and leveraging opportunities, healthcare organizations can harness the power of AI-enhanced telehealth to drive innovation and improve patient outcomes. The future of healthcare lies in the seamless integration of AI and telehealth, and with careful planning and execution, its full potential can be realized.

Bibliography

Aidoc. (n.d.). "Radiology AI imaging — Faster, smarter care." https://www.aidoc.com/solutions/radiology/

Deep Genomics, Inc. (n.d.). "Deep genomics — AI platform for genomic medicine." https://www.deepgenomics.com/AI-Platform/

Fitzpatrick, K. K., Darcy, A., & Vierhile, M. (2017). "Delivering cognitive behavior therapy to young adults with symptoms of depression and anxiety using a fully automated conversational agent (Woebot): A randomized controlled trial." JMIR Mental Health, 4(2), e19. https://doi.org/10.2196/mental.7785 — https://mental.jmir.org/2017/2/e19/ — company: https://woebothealth.com/

PathAI, Inc. (n.d.). "PathAI — Pathology transformed." https://www.pathai.com/

Perez, M. V., Mahaffey, K. W., Hedlin, H., Rumsfeld, J. S., Garcia, A., Ferris, T., Balasubramanian, V., Russo, A. M., Rajmane, A., Cheung, L., Hung, G., Lee, J., Kowey, P., Talati, N., Nag, D., Gummidipundi, S. E., Beatty, A., Hills, M. T., Desai, S., … Turakhia, M. P. (2019). "Large-scale assessment of a smartwatch to identify atrial fibrillation." New England Journal of Medicine, 381(20), 1909–1917. https://doi.org/10.1056/NEJMoa1901183

Teladoc Health, Inc. (2020, August 5). *Teladoc Health and Livongo merge to create new standard in global healthcare delivery, access and experience* [Press release]. https://ir.teladoc.com/news-and-events/investor-news/press-release-details/2020/Teladoc-Health-and-Livongo-Merge-with-Livongo/default.aspx

Tempus AI, Inc. (n.d.). "Tempus — AI-powered precision medicine and genomic testing." https://www.tempus.com/

Chapter 15

Preparing for the Workforce of Tomorrow: AI in Medical Education

As Artificial Intelligence (AI) continues to reshape the landscape of healthcare, preparing the next generation of healthcare professionals to work with AI is crucial. Medical education must evolve to incorporate AI training, ensuring that future doctors, nurses, and healthcare administrators are equipped with the skills and knowledge to harness the power of AI. This chapter explores how AI is being integrated into medical education, the challenges and opportunities it presents, and practical strategies for training the workforce of tomorrow.

The Need for AI Training in Medical Education

The integration of AI in healthcare is creating a paradigm shift that requires healthcare professionals to understand and effectively use AI tools. To achieve this, medical

DOI: 10.4324/9781003571407-20

education must adapt to include AI training as a core component.

The Evolving Role of Healthcare Professionals

AI is not intended to replace healthcare professionals but to augment their capabilities. Understanding how to collaborate with AI systems will be essential for delivering high-quality patient care.

Example: AI-Assisted Diagnostics. Future doctors will need to interpret AI-generated diagnostic insights, understand the underlying algorithms, and integrate AI recommendations with their clinical judgment.

Outcomes:

- **Enhanced Decision-Making:** AI training will enable healthcare professionals to make more informed decisions by leveraging AI insights.
- **Improved Patient Outcomes:** Combining AI capabilities with clinical expertise can lead to better patient outcomes through more accurate diagnoses and personalized treatments.

Key Takeaway: AI training is essential for empowering healthcare professionals to harness AI tools effectively and improve patient care.

Integrating AI into Medical Curricula

To prepare the workforce of tomorrow, medical schools and training programs must integrate AI education into their curricula. This includes both theoretical knowledge and practical applications.

Curriculum Development

Developing a comprehensive AI curriculum involves collaboration between medical educators, AI experts, and industry partners. The curriculum should cover foundational AI concepts, ethical considerations, and hands-on experience with AI tools.

Example: Stanford University School of Medicine. Stanford University has incorporated AI into its medical curriculum, offering courses on machine learning, data science, and AI ethics. Students also have access to AI labs where they can work on real-world projects.

Outcomes:

- **Comprehensive Education:** Students receive a well-rounded education that includes both theoretical knowledge and practical experience with AI.
- **Industry Collaboration:** Partnerships with AI companies provide students with exposure to cutting-edge technologies and industry practices.

Key Takeaway: Integrating AI into medical curricula prepares students to work effectively with AI technologies in their future careers.

Practical AI Training and Simulation

In addition to classroom learning, practical AI training and simulation are critical for developing the skills needed to work with AI in clinical settings.

Use Case: AI-Driven Simulations

AI-driven simulations provide a safe and controlled environment for students to practice using AI tools. These simulations can replicate real-world scenarios, allowing students to learn how to interpret AI-generated data and make clinical decisions.

Example: University of Toronto. The University of Toronto uses AI-driven simulations to train medical students in diagnostic radiology. The simulations provide realistic scenarios where students can practice interpreting AI-generated imaging results and integrating them with clinical information.

Outcomes:

- **Hands-On Experience:** Students gain practical experience with AI tools, enhancing their confidence and competence.
- **Safe Learning Environment:** Simulations offer a risk-free environment where students can learn from mistakes and improve their skills.

Key Takeaway: AI-driven simulations provide valuable hands-on experience, preparing students to use AI tools effectively in clinical practice.

Addressing Challenges and Opportunities

Integrating AI into medical education presents both challenges and opportunities that must be addressed to ensure successful implementation.

Challenges:

1. **Resource Constraints:** Developing and implementing AI curricula requires significant resources, including funding, faculty training, and access to technology.
2. **Faculty Expertise:** Medical educators may need additional training to teach AI concepts effectively, requiring investment in professional development.

3. **Curriculum Integration:** Balancing AI education with existing medical curricula can be challenging, necessitating careful planning and coordination.

Opportunities:

1. **Enhanced Learning:** AI can enhance medical education by providing personalized learning experiences and adaptive assessments tailored to individual student needs.
2. **Interdisciplinary Collaboration:** Integrating AI into medical education fosters collaboration between medical and AI experts, leading to innovative teaching methods and research opportunities.
3. **Future-Ready Workforce:** Preparing students to work with AI ensures that the future healthcare workforce is equipped to leverage AI technologies, driving innovation and improving patient care.

Practical Do's and Don'ts for Integrating AI into Medical Education

Do's:

1. **Do Collaborate with AI Experts:** Partner with AI experts and industry leaders to develop comprehensive and up-to-date AI curricula.
2. **Do Invest in Faculty Development:** Provide training and resources for faculty to ensure they are equipped to teach AI concepts effectively.
3. **Do Incorporate Hands-On Training:** Use AI-driven simulations and practical exercises to give students hands-on experience with AI tools.
4. **Do Address Ethical Considerations:** Include AI ethics as a core component of the curriculum to ensure students understand the ethical implications of AI in healthcare.

5. **Do Foster a Culture of Innovation:** Encourage students to explore AI applications and contribute to AI research and development.

Don'ts:

1. **Don't Neglect Interdisciplinary Learning:** Ensure that AI education is interdisciplinary, involving collaboration between medical, data science, and engineering faculties.
2. **Don't Overlook the Importance of Data Quality:** Teach students the importance of high-quality data for training accurate AI models and the potential consequences of biased data.
3. **Don't Ignore Student Feedback:** Gather and incorporate feedback from students to continuously improve AI curricula and training programs.
4. **Don't Underestimate the Complexity of AI:** Provide a balanced education that covers both the capabilities and limitations of AI, setting realistic expectations.
5. **Don't Skimp on Resources:** Allocate sufficient resources to ensure the successful implementation and sustainability of AI education programs.

Conclusion

Integrating AI into medical education is essential for preparing the healthcare workforce of tomorrow. By developing comprehensive curricula, providing practical training, and addressing challenges and opportunities, medical schools can ensure that future healthcare professionals are equipped to harness the power of AI. This preparation will enable them to deliver high-quality patient care, drive innovation, and lead the healthcare industry into a new era of AI-driven excellence.

Bibliography

Fitzpatrick, K. K., Darcy, A., & Vierhile, M. (2017). "Delivering cognitive behavior therapy to young adults with symptoms of depression and anxiety using a fully automated conversational agent (Woebot): A randomized controlled trial." JMIR Mental Health, 4(2), e19. https://doi.org/10.2196/mental.7785 — company: https://woebothealth.com/

Stanford Center for Artificial Intelligence in Medicine and Imaging (AIMI). (n.d.). "Education — AIMI." https://aimi.stanford.edu/education

Teladoc Health, Inc. (2020, August 5). *Teladoc Health and Livongo merge to create new standard in global healthcare delivery, access and experience* [Press release]. https://ir.teladoc.com/news-and-events/investor-news/press-release-details/2020/Teladoc-Health-and-Livongo-Merge-with-Livongo/default.aspx

Temerty Centre for Artificial Intelligence Research and Education in Medicine (T-CAIREM), University of Toronto. (n.d.). "T-CAIREM — AI research and education in medicine." https://tcairem.utoronto.ca/

Tempus AI, Inc. (n.d.). "Tempus — AI-powered precision medicine and genomic testing." https://www.tempus.com/

Chapter 16

AI in Global Health: Bridging the Healthcare Divide

Artificial Intelligence (AI) has the potential to bridge the healthcare divide, offering solutions to some of the most pressing global health challenges. By leveraging AI technologies, healthcare can become more accessible, efficient, and equitable, particularly in underserved and low-resource settings. This chapter explores how AI is transforming global health, with real-world examples, challenges, opportunities, and practical strategies for implementation.

The Global Health Divide

Healthcare disparities are a significant global issue, with vast differences in healthcare access and quality between high-income and low-income countries. These disparities are often exacerbated by factors such as poverty, limited infrastructure, and shortages of healthcare professionals.

DOI: 10.4324/9781003571407-21

The Challenges of Global Health:

1. **Limited Access to Healthcare:** Many low-income countries face significant barriers to accessing healthcare, including geographic isolation, inadequate infrastructure, and financial constraints.
2. **Shortage of Healthcare Professionals:** A critical shortage of healthcare workers, particularly in rural and remote areas, limits the availability of medical care.
3. **Inadequate Infrastructure:** Poor infrastructure, including unreliable electricity and internet connectivity, hampers the delivery of healthcare services.
4. **Disease Burden:** High prevalence of infectious diseases, coupled with emerging non-communicable diseases, places a significant burden on healthcare systems.

AI Solutions for Global Health

AI has the potential to address many of these challenges by improving diagnostics, streamlining operations, and enabling remote care. Here are some ways AI is being used to transform global health.

Use Case: AI-Powered Diagnostics

AI can enhance diagnostic accuracy and speed, particularly in low-resource settings where access to specialist care is limited.

Example: Google AI and Tuberculosis Detection. Google AI developed an AI model to detect tuberculosis (TB) from chest X-rays. This tool is particularly valuable in low-resource settings where radiologists are scarce.

Outcomes:

- **Increased Accuracy:** The AI model demonstrated high accuracy in detecting TB, comparable to that of expert radiologists.
- **Scalability:** The tool can be deployed widely, providing diagnostic support in areas with limited access to radiologists.
- **Early Detection:** Early and accurate detection of TB enables timely treatment, reducing transmission and improving patient outcomes.

Key Takeaway: AI-powered diagnostics can enhance the accuracy and accessibility of medical diagnoses in low-resource settings, improving health outcomes.

Use Case: Remote Health Monitoring and Telemedicine

AI can facilitate remote health monitoring and telemedicine, bringing healthcare services to patients in remote and underserved areas.

Example: Zipline and Drone Delivery of Medical Supplies. Zipline uses AI-powered drones to deliver medical supplies, such as blood and vaccines, to remote areas in Rwanda and Ghana. AI algorithms optimize flight paths and delivery schedules.

Outcomes:

- **Improved Access:** The drone delivery system ensures that essential medical supplies reach remote areas quickly and efficiently.
- **Reduced Mortality:** Timely delivery of medical supplies has led to a reduction in mortality rates, particularly for postpartum hemorrhage.

- **Operational Efficiency:** AI optimizes logistics, reducing delivery times and costs.

Key Takeaway: AI-enabled logistics and telemedicine can bridge the gap in healthcare access for remote and underserved populations.

Use Case: AI in Disease Surveillance and Outbreak Prediction

AI can analyze large datasets to predict disease outbreaks and monitor the spread of infectious diseases, enabling proactive public health responses.

Example: BlueDot and COVID-19. BlueDot, a Canadian health monitoring company, uses AI to track and predict the spread of infectious diseases. BlueDot's AI platform detected the COVID-19 outbreak in Wuhan, China, days before official announcements.

Outcomes:

- **Early Warning:** The AI system provided early warnings about the outbreak, allowing for quicker public health interventions.
- **Data Integration:** The platform integrates data from various sources, including news reports, airline data, and public health databases.
- **Global Reach:** BlueDot's AI platform monitors disease outbreaks globally, providing valuable insights for public health officials.

Key Takeaway: AI-driven disease surveillance and outbreak prediction can enhance global health security by enabling early detection and response to infectious diseases.

Challenges and Opportunities

While AI offers significant promise for global health, several challenges must be addressed to ensure successful implementation.

Challenges:

1. **Data Quality and Availability:** High-quality data is essential for training accurate AI models, but data collection in low-resource settings can be challenging due to limited infrastructure and resources.
2. **Infrastructure Limitations:** Inadequate infrastructure, including unreliable electricity and internet connectivity, can hinder the deployment and use of AI technologies.
3. **Cultural and Ethical Considerations:** AI solutions must be culturally sensitive and ethically sound, ensuring that they respect local norms and values.
4. **Capacity Building:** Building local capacity to develop, implement, and maintain AI systems is crucial for sustainability and long-term success.

Opportunities:

1. **Scalable Solutions:** AI offers scalable solutions that can be deployed widely, providing healthcare services to large populations in low-resource settings.
2. **Cost-Effective Interventions:** AI can reduce healthcare costs by streamlining operations, optimizing resource allocation, and improving efficiency.
3. **Empowerment of Local Communities:** Training and empowering local healthcare workers to use AI technologies can enhance their capacity to deliver high-quality care.
4. **Global Collaboration:** International collaboration and partnerships can drive the development and deployment of AI solutions, leveraging global expertise and resources.

Practical Do's and Don'ts for Implementing AI in Global Health

Do's:

1. **Do Prioritize Data Quality:** Invest in data collection and curation processes to ensure high-quality data for training AI models.
2. **Do Build Local Capacity:** Provide training and resources to local healthcare workers to ensure they can effectively use and maintain AI systems.
3. **Do Collaborate with Local Stakeholders:** Engage local communities, healthcare providers, and policymakers in the development and implementation of AI solutions to ensure they meet local needs and contexts.
4. **Do Address Ethical Considerations:** Ensure that AI solutions are culturally sensitive, ethically sound, and respect local norms and values.
5. **Do Focus on Sustainability:** Develop sustainable AI solutions that can be maintained and scaled over the long term, providing lasting benefits to local communities.

Don'ts:

1. **Don't Ignore Infrastructure Limitations:** Consider the infrastructure constraints in low-resource settings and develop AI solutions that can function effectively within these limitations.
2. **Don't Overlook Local Context:** Ensure that AI solutions are tailored to the specific needs and contexts of the populations they serve, avoiding a one-size-fits-all approach.
3. **Don't Neglect Regulatory Compliance:** Ensure that AI solutions comply with local regulations and standards to avoid legal and ethical issues.
4. **Don't Underestimate the Importance of Trust:** Build trust with local communities by being transparent

about the capabilities and limitations of AI solutions and involving them in the decision-making process.

5. **Don't Forget Continuous Monitoring and Evaluation:** Continuously monitor and evaluate AI solutions to identify issues, gather feedback, and make iterative improvements.

Conclusion

AI has the potential to transform global health by bridging the healthcare divide and offering scalable, cost-effective solutions to some of the world's most pressing health challenges. By addressing the challenges and leveraging the opportunities presented by AI, healthcare organizations can improve access to care, enhance diagnostic accuracy, and strengthen public health responses in low-resource settings. The future of global health lies in the successful integration of AI technologies, and with careful planning and execution, its transformative potential can be fully realized.

Bibliography

Aidoc. (n.d.). "Radiology AI imaging — Faster, smarter care." https://www.aidoc.com/solutions/radiology/

Bogoch, I. I., Watts, A., Thomas-Bachli, A., Huber, C., Kraemer, M. U. G., & Khan, K. (2020). "Pneumonia of unknown aetiology in Wuhan, China: Potential for international spread via commercial air travel." Journal of Travel Medicine, 27(2), taaa008. https://doi.org/10.1093/jtm/taaa008 (BlueDot early warning for COVID-19; Khan is BlueDot's founder.) — company: https://bluedot.global/

Deep Genomics, Inc. (n.d.). "Deep Genomics — AI platform for genomic medicine." https://www.deepgenomics.com/AI-Platform/

Fitzpatrick, K. K., Darcy, A., & Vierhile, M. (2017). "Delivering cognitive behavior therapy to young adults with symptoms of depression and anxiety using a fully automated conversational agent (Woebot): A randomized controlled trial." JMIR Mental Health, 4(2), e19. https://doi.org/10.2196/mental.7785

Nabulsi, Z., Sellergren, A., Jamshy, S., Lau, C., Santos, E., Kiraly, A. P., Ye, W., Yang, J., Pilgrim, R., Kazemzadeh, S., Yu, J., Kalidindi, S. R., Etemadi, M., Garcia-Vicente, F., Melnick, D., Corrado, G. S., Peng, L., Eswaran, K., Tse, D., … Shetty, S. (2021). "Deep learning for distinguishing normal versus abnormal chest radiographs and generalization to two unseen diseases tuberculosis and COVID-19." Scientific Reports, 11, 15523. https://doi.org/10.1038/s41598-021-93967-2 (Google Health)

PathAI, Inc. (n.d.). "PathAI — Pathology transformed." https://www.pathai.com/

Perez, M. V., Mahaffey, K. W., Hedlin, H., Rumsfeld, J. S., Garcia, A., Ferris, T., Balasubramanian, V., Russo, A. M., Rajmane, A., Cheung, L., Hung, G., Lee, J., Kowey, P., Talati, N., Nag, D., Gummidipundi, S. E., Beatty, A., Hills, M. T., Desai, S., … Turakhia, M. P. (2019). "Large-scale assessment of a smartwatch to identify atrial fibrillation." New England Journal of Medicine, 381(20), 1909–1917. https://doi.org/10.1056/NEJMoa1901183

Teladoc Health, Inc. (2020, August 5). "Teladoc Health and Livongo merge to create new standard in global healthcare delivery, access and experience [Press release]." https://ir.teladochealth.com/news-and-events/investor-news/press-release-details/2020/Teladoc-Health-and-Livongo-Merge-to-Create-New-Standard-in-Global-Healthcare-Delivery-Access-and-Experience/default.aspx

Tempus AI, Inc. (n.d.). "Tempus — AI-powered precision medicine and genomic testing." https://www.tempus.com/

Zipline International Inc. (n.d.). "Zipline — Instant delivery, at scale." https://www.zipline.com/

Chapter 17

The Economic Impact of AI in Healthcare

Artificial Intelligence (AI) is poised to bring transformative changes to healthcare, not just in terms of patient outcomes but also in economic aspects. The integration of AI in healthcare has the potential to significantly reduce costs, improve efficiency, and drive innovation. This chapter explores the economic impact of AI in healthcare, discussing cost savings, new revenue streams, workforce implications, and the overall value AI brings to the healthcare industry.

Cost Savings through AI Integration

One of the most compelling economic benefits of AI in healthcare is its potential to reduce costs across various domains. By automating routine tasks, improving diagnostics, and optimizing operations, AI can lead to substantial cost savings.

DOI: 10.4324/9781003571407-22

Use Case: Reducing Administrative Costs

Example: Optum. Optum, a health services company, uses AI to streamline administrative processes such as billing and claims processing. AI algorithms automate the verification of claims, detect errors, and prevent fraudulent activities.

Outcomes:

- **Efficiency:** Automation reduces the time and labor required for administrative tasks.
- **Accuracy:** AI improves the accuracy of claims processing, reducing errors and rework.
- **Cost Savings:** The reduction in administrative overheads leads to significant cost savings.

Key Takeaway: AI can streamline administrative processes, reducing labor costs and increasing operational efficiency.

Use Case: Optimizing Resource Utilization

Example: Cleveland Clinic. Cleveland Clinic implemented an AI-driven system to optimize the scheduling of surgeries and allocation of operating rooms. The AI system analyzes historical data to predict surgery durations and patient recovery times, enabling more efficient use of resources.

Outcomes:

- **Resource Optimization:** Improved scheduling reduces idle time for operating rooms and ensures optimal use of medical staff.
- **Cost Efficiency:** Better resource utilization leads to cost savings by maximizing the productivity of existing assets.
- **Patient Throughput:** Enhanced scheduling increases the number of surgeries that can be performed, boosting revenue.

Key Takeaway: AI-driven resource optimization can lead to better utilization of healthcare facilities and staff, resulting in cost savings and increased revenue.

Generating New Revenue Streams

In addition to cost savings, AI can create new revenue streams for healthcare organizations by enabling innovative services and enhancing existing offerings.

Use Case: AI-Powered Health Monitoring Services

Example: Fitbit. Fitbit, a company known for its wearable health devices, uses AI to offer personalized health insights and coaching services. By analyzing data from wearable devices, AI provides users with tailored health recommendations and fitness plans.

Outcomes:

- **Subscription Revenue:** Personalized health services generate recurring subscription revenue.
- **User Engagement:** AI-driven insights enhance user engagement and retention.
- **Market Differentiation:** Offering AI-powered services differentiates Fitbit in a competitive market.

Key Takeaway: AI enables healthcare organizations to offer personalized health services, creating new revenue streams through subscription models and enhanced customer engagement.

Use Case: AI in Drug Discovery and Development

Example: Insilico Medicine. Insilico Medicine uses AI to accelerate drug discovery by predicting the efficacy of new compounds and identifying potential drug candidates. This AI-driven approach reduces the time and cost associated with traditional drug development.

Outcomes:

- **Faster Time-to-Market:** AI accelerates the drug development process, bringing new drugs to market more quickly.
- **Cost Reduction:** Reduced research and development costs increase profitability.
- **Partnership Opportunities:** Collaboration with pharmaceutical companies generates additional revenue through partnerships and licensing deals.

Key Takeaway: AI in drug discovery can reduce development costs and time, creating new revenue opportunities through faster market entry and industry partnerships.

Workforce Implications

The integration of AI in healthcare also has significant implications for the workforce. While AI can automate certain tasks, it also creates opportunities for new roles and enhances the capabilities of existing staff.

Enhancing Workforce Productivity

AI tools can augment the capabilities of healthcare professionals, enabling them to focus on higher-value tasks and improve productivity.

Example: AI-Assisted Radiology. Radiologists using AI tools for image analysis can quickly identify abnormalities, allowing them to focus on complex cases that require expert interpretation.

Outcomes:

- **Efficiency:** AI reduces the time spent on routine image analysis.
- **Accuracy:** Enhanced diagnostic accuracy improves patient outcomes.
- **Job Satisfaction:** Radiologists can focus on more challenging and rewarding tasks.

Key Takeaway: AI can enhance workforce productivity by automating routine tasks and enabling healthcare professionals to focus on higher-value activities.

Creating New Job Opportunities

The rise of AI in healthcare also creates new job opportunities in areas such as AI system development, data management, and cybersecurity.

Example: AI in Healthcare Informatics The demand for healthcare informaticians who can manage and analyze large datasets is growing. These professionals play a crucial role in developing and maintaining AI systems.

Outcomes:

- **Job Creation:** New roles in AI system development, data management, and analysis are created.
- **Skill Development:** Workforce training and development programs help existing staff acquire new skills.
- **Innovation:** A skilled workforce drives innovation and the development of advanced AI solutions.

Key Takeaway: AI creates new job opportunities and drives the need for continuous skill development and training.

Overall Value of AI in Healthcare

The integration of AI in healthcare brings overall value by improving patient outcomes, enhancing operational efficiency, and driving innovation. The economic impact of AI extends beyond cost savings and revenue generation to include broader societal benefits.

Improving Patient Outcomes

AI improves patient outcomes through early diagnosis, personalized treatment, and continuous monitoring.

Example: Personalized Medicine. AI-driven personalized medicine tailors treatments to individual patients, improving efficacy and reducing adverse effects.

Outcomes:

- **Better Health Outcomes:** Personalized treatments lead to improved patient health.
- **Cost Savings:** Reduced hospital readmissions and complications lower healthcare costs.
- **Patient Satisfaction:** Improved health outcomes enhance patient satisfaction and trust.

Key Takeaway: AI-driven personalized medicine improves patient outcomes and reduces healthcare costs.

Enhancing Operational Efficiency

AI streamlines healthcare operations, reducing waste and optimizing resource use.

Example: Hospital Workflow Optimization. AI systems optimize hospital workflows by predicting patient admissions, discharges, and staff requirements.

Outcomes:

- **Operational Efficiency:** Optimized workflows reduce waiting times and improve patient flow.
- **Cost Reduction:** Efficient operations lower operational costs.
- **Quality of Care:** Streamlined processes enhance the overall quality of care.

Key Takeaway: AI-driven workflow optimization improves operational efficiency and the quality of healthcare delivery.

Driving Innovation

AI fosters innovation in healthcare by enabling new treatments, improving existing processes, and supporting cutting-edge research.

Example: AI in Genomic Research. AI analyzes genomic data to identify genetic markers for diseases, supporting the development of targeted therapies.

Outcomes:

- **Scientific Advances:** AI accelerates research and the discovery of new treatments.
- **Healthcare Innovation:** Innovative AI solutions transform healthcare delivery.
- **Economic Growth:** Investment in AI research and development drives economic growth in the healthcare sector.

Key Takeaway: AI drives innovation in healthcare, leading to scientific advances and economic growth.

Practical Do's and Don'ts for Leveraging AI's Economic Impact

Do's:

1. **Do Invest in AI Infrastructure:** Allocate resources to develop and maintain robust AI infrastructure, including data management systems and computing power.
2. **Do Foster a Culture of Innovation:** Encourage a culture of innovation by supporting AI research and development and promoting collaboration between AI experts and healthcare professionals.
3. **Do Focus on Workforce Training:** Provide training and development programs to help healthcare professionals acquire AI-related skills and adapt to new roles.
4. **Do Measure Economic Impact:** Continuously measure and evaluate the economic impact of AI initiatives to identify areas for improvement and demonstrate value.
5. **Do Engage Stakeholders:** Involve stakeholders, including healthcare providers, patients, and policymakers, in the development and implementation of AI solutions.

Don'ts:

1. **Don't Overlook Data Quality:** Ensure high-quality data is used for training AI models to avoid inaccurate predictions and suboptimal outcomes.
2. **Don't Ignore Ethical Considerations:** Address ethical issues, such as bias and privacy, to build trust and ensure the responsible use of AI.
3. **Don't Neglect Regulatory Compliance:** Stay informed about regulatory requirements and ensure AI solutions comply with relevant standards and regulations.

4. **Don't Underestimate Integration Challenges:** Plan for the integration of AI with existing systems and workflows to avoid disruptions and maximize benefits.
5. **Don't Focus Solely on Cost Savings:** Consider the broader value of AI, including improvements in patient outcomes, operational efficiency, and innovation.

Conclusion

The economic impact of AI in healthcare is profound, offering cost savings, new revenue streams, workforce enhancements, and overall value. By strategically investing in AI infrastructure, fostering innovation, and focusing on workforce development, healthcare organizations can harness the full potential of AI to drive economic growth and improve healthcare delivery. The future of healthcare is intertwined with AI, and with thoughtful planning and execution, its transformative economic impact can be fully realized.

Bibliography

Bogoch, I. I., Watts, A., Thomas-Bachli, A., Huber, C., Kraemer, M. U. G., & Khan, K. (2020). "Pneumonia of unknown aetiology in Wuhan, China: Potential for international spread via commercial air travel." Journal of Travel Medicine, 27(2), taaa008. https://doi.org/10.1093/jtm/taaa008 (BlueDot)

Fitzpatrick, K. K., Darcy, A., & Vierhile, M. (2017). "Delivering cognitive behavior therapy to young adults with symptoms of depression and anxiety using a fully automated conversational agent (Woebot): A randomized controlled trial." JMIR Mental Health, 4(2), e19. https://doi.org/10.2196/mental.7785

Lubitz, S. A., Faranesh, A. Z., Selvaggi, C., Atlas, S. J., McManus, D. D., Singer, D. E., Pagoto, S., McConnell, M. V., Pantelopoulos, A., & Foulkes, A. S. (2022). "Detection of atrial fibrillation in a large population using wearable devices: The Fitbit Heart Study." Circulation, 146(19), 1415–1424. https://doi.org/10.1161/CIRCULATIONAHA.122.060291

PathAI, Inc. (n.d.). "PathAI — Pathology transformed." https://www.pathai.com/

Perez, M. V., Mahaffey, K. W., Hedlin, H., Rumsfeld, J. S., Garcia, A., Ferris, T., Balasubramanian, V., Russo, A. M., Rajmane, A., Cheung, L., Hung, G., Lee, J., Kowey, P., Talati, N., Nag, D., Gummidipundi, S. E., Beatty, A., Hills, M. T., Desai, S., … Turakhia, M. P. (2019). "Large-scale assessment of a smartwatch to identify atrial fibrillation." New England Journal of Medicine, 381(20), 1909–1917. https://doi.org/10.1056/NEJMoa1901183

Teladoc Health, Inc. (2020, August 5). "Teladoc Health and Livongo merge to create new standard in global healthcare delivery, access and experience [Press release]." https://ir.teladochealth.com/news-and-events/investor-news/press-release-details/2020/Teladoc-Health-and-Livongo-Merge-to-Create-New-Standard-in-Global-Healthcare-Delivery-Access-and-Experience/default.aspx

Tempus AI, Inc. (n.d.). "Tempus — AI-powered precision medicine and genomic testing." https://www.tempus.com/

UnitedHealth Group / Optum. (n.d.). "Making health care work smarter, for everyone — Artificial intelligence." https://www.unitedhealthgroup.com/uhg/what-we-do/artificial-intelligence.html

Zhavoronkov, A., Ivanenkov, Y. A., Aliper, A., Veselov, M. S., Aladinskiy, V. A., Aladinskaya, A. V., Terentiev, V. A., Polykovskiy, D. A., Kuznetsov, M. D., Asadulaev, A., Volkov, Y., Zholus, A., Shayakhmetov, R. R., Zhebrak, A., Minaeva, L. I., Zagribelnyy, B. A., Lee, L. H., Soll, R., Madge, D., … Aspuru-Guzik, A. (2019). "Deep learning enables rapid identification of potent DDR1 kinase inhibitors." Nature Biotechnology, 37(9), 1038–1040. https://doi.org/10.1038/s41587-019-0224-x (Insilico Medicine) — company: https://insilico.com/

Chapter 18

Ethical AI: Balancing Innovation with Responsibility

Artificial Intelligence (AI) holds immense promise for transforming healthcare, but it also raises important ethical questions. Balancing innovation with responsibility is crucial to ensure that AI technologies are developed and deployed in ways that are fair, transparent, and beneficial to all. This chapter delves into the ethical considerations surrounding AI in healthcare, discussing key issues, real-world examples, and strategies for developing and implementing ethical AI solutions.

The Importance of Ethical AI

Ethical AI involves creating and using AI systems in ways that respect human rights, promote fairness, and ensure accountability. In healthcare, ethical AI is particularly critical due to the direct impact on patient health and well-being.

DOI: 10.4324/9781003571407-23

Key Ethical Issues in AI:

1. **Bias and Fairness:** AI systems can inadvertently perpetuate biases present in the training data, leading to unfair and discriminatory outcomes.
2. **Transparency and Explainability:** AI systems often operate as "black boxes," making it difficult for users to understand how decisions are made. Transparency and explainability are essential for building trust.
3. **Privacy and Data Security:** The use of large datasets in AI raises concerns about patient privacy and data security, requiring robust protections and compliance with regulations.
4. **Accountability:** Determining responsibility when AI systems fail or cause harm is a significant ethical challenge, necessitating clear accountability frameworks.
5. **Access and Equity:** Ensuring that the benefits of AI are accessible to all, including underserved and marginalized populations, is crucial for promoting health equity.

Real-World Examples of Ethical AI Challenges

Example: Bias in Predictive Algorithms

Case Study: COMPAS Algorithm The Correctional Offender Management Profiling for Alternative Sanctions (COMPAS) algorithm, used in the criminal justice system to predict recidivism, has faced criticism for racial bias. Studies have shown that COMPAS is more likely to incorrectly predict higher recidivism risk for Black defendants compared to white defendants (Angwin et al., 2016).

Outcomes:

- **Bias Awareness:** The case highlighted the need for rigorous bias testing in AI systems.

- **Policy Changes:** There have been calls for greater transparency and accountability in the use of predictive algorithms in criminal justice.

Key Takeaway: Bias in AI can have serious consequences, underscoring the importance of developing fair and unbiased AI systems.

Example: Lack of Explainability in AI Diagnostics

Case Study: IBM Watson for Oncology IBM Watson for Oncology, an AI system designed to assist oncologists in developing cancer treatment plans, faced challenges due to its lack of transparency and explainability. Oncologists reported difficulty understanding how the AI arrived at its recommendations, leading to skepticism and limited adoption (Ross & Swetlitz, 2017).

Outcomes:

- **Limited Adoption:** The lack of explainability hindered the system's acceptance among healthcare professionals.
- **Revised Approaches:** IBM has since focused on improving the transparency and explainability of its AI solutions.

Key Takeaway: Transparency and explainability are crucial for gaining user trust and ensuring the effective use of AI in clinical settings.

Strategies for Developing and Implementing Ethical AI

To address these ethical challenges, healthcare organizations and AI developers must adopt strategies that prioritize fairness, transparency, accountability, and equity.

Ensuring Fairness and Mitigating Bias:

1. **Diverse Datasets:** Use diverse and representative datasets to train AI models, ensuring that they reflect the populations they serve.
2. **Bias Audits:** Conduct regular bias audits to identify and address biases in AI models. This involves analyzing outcomes across different demographic groups.
3. **Inclusive Development:** Involve diverse stakeholders, including ethicists, patients, and community representatives, in the development and evaluation of AI systems.

Example: Google Health. Google Health has implemented rigorous bias testing protocols to ensure that its AI systems, such as those for detecting diabetic retinopathy, perform equitably across different demographic groups (Gulshan et al., 2016).

Outcomes:

- **Fairer Systems:** AI systems that are more equitable and perform well across diverse populations.
- **Improved Trust:** Increased trust in AI solutions due to demonstrated fairness and equity.

Key Takeaway: Ensuring fairness and mitigating bias are essential for developing ethical AI systems that serve all populations equitably.

Promoting Transparency and Explainability:

1. **Explainable AI (XAI):** Develop AI models that provide clear and understandable explanations for their decisions. This helps users understand how outcomes are derived.
2. **User Training:** Educate users on how AI systems work, including their capabilities and limitations, to build confidence and trust.

3. **Open Communication:** Maintain open communication with stakeholders about the AI development process, including data sources, methodologies, and potential biases.

Example: DARPA XAI Program The Defense Advanced Research Projects Agency (DARPA) launched the XAI program to create AI systems that are both high-performing and interpretable by humans. The program focuses on developing techniques that allow AI systems to explain their decisions in ways that are understandable to users (Gunning, 2017).

Outcomes:

- **Improved Interpretability:** AI systems that provide clear explanations for their decisions.
- **Enhanced Trust:** Greater user trust and acceptance of AI systems due to improved transparency.

Key Takeaway: Transparency and explainability are critical for ethical AI, helping to build user trust and facilitate informed decision-making.

Protecting Privacy and Data Security:

1. **Robust Security Measures:** Implement robust data security measures, including encryption, access controls, and regular security audits, to protect patient data.
2. **Compliance with Regulations:** Ensure compliance with data protection regulations, such as the General Data Protection Regulation (GDPR) and the Health Insurance Portability and Accountability Act (HIPAA).
3. **Data Minimization:** Use data minimization techniques to limit the amount of personal data collected and processed by AI systems.

Example: Mayo Clinic and Google Cloud Partnership. Mayo Clinic partnered with Google Cloud to develop AI solutions for healthcare while ensuring stringent data privacy and security measures. The collaboration involves advanced encryption techniques and strict access controls to protect patient data (Mayo Clinic, 2019).

Outcomes:

- **Enhanced Privacy:** Robust data privacy protections that comply with regulatory standards
- **Trustworthy AI:** Increased trust in AI solutions due to strong privacy and security measures.

Key Takeaway: Protecting privacy and data security is essential for ethical AI, ensuring patient trust and compliance with regulations.

Establishing Accountability Frameworks:

1. **Clear Accountability Structures:** Define clear accountability structures that specify who is responsible for AI decisions and outcomes.
2. **Ethical Guidelines:** Develop and adhere to ethical guidelines that outline the principles and standards for AI development and deployment.
3. **Continuous Monitoring:** Implement continuous monitoring and evaluation processes to ensure AI systems perform as intended and to identify and address any issues promptly.

Example: Microsoft AI Ethics Committee. Microsoft established an AI ethics committee to oversee the development and deployment of AI technologies. The committee ensures that AI solutions adhere to ethical guidelines and principles, such as fairness, transparency, and accountability (Smith & Shum, 2018).

Outcomes:

- **Ethical Oversight:** Structured oversight of AI development and deployment to ensure ethical practices.
- **Responsibility:** Clear accountability for AI decisions and outcomes.

Key Takeaway: Establishing accountability frameworks is crucial for ethical AI, ensuring responsible development and deployment of AI technologies.

Practical Do's and Don'ts for Ethical AI in Healthcare

Do's:

1. **Do Conduct Bias Audits:** Regularly audit AI systems for biases and take corrective actions to ensure fairness.
2. **Do Promote Transparency:** Develop AI systems that are transparent and provide clear explanations for their decisions.
3. **Do Protect Privacy:** Implement robust data privacy and security measures to protect patient information.
4. **Do Establish Accountability:** Define clear accountability structures and adhere to ethical guidelines to ensure responsible AI development.
5. **Do Engage Stakeholders:** Involve diverse stakeholders in the AI development process to ensure multiple perspectives are considered.

Don'ts:

1. **Don't Ignore Bias:** Failing to address bias in AI systems can lead to unfair and harmful outcomes.
2. **Don't Neglect Explainability:** Lack of transparency and explainability can undermine trust and hinder the adoption of AI solutions.

3. **Don't Overlook Privacy:** Neglecting data privacy and security can lead to breaches and loss of trust.
4. **Don't Skimp on Accountability:** Lack of clear accountability can result in ethical lapses and harm to patients.
5. **Don't Exclude Stakeholders:** Excluding stakeholders from the AI development process can result in systems that do not meet user needs or ethical standards.

Conclusion

Balancing innovation with responsibility is essential for the ethical development and deployment of AI in healthcare. By addressing key ethical issues such as bias, transparency, privacy, and accountability, healthcare organizations can ensure that AI technologies are developed and used in ways that are fair, transparent, and beneficial to all. The future of ethical AI in healthcare depends on our commitment to these principles, ensuring that AI serves as a force for good in transforming patient care.

Bibliography

Angwin, J., Larson, J., Mattu, S., & Kirchner, L. (2016, May 23). "Machine bias: There's software used across the country to predict future criminals. And it's biased against blacks." ProPublica. https://www.propublica.org/article/machine-bias-risk-assessments-in-criminal-sentencing

Gulshan, V., Peng, L., Coram, M., Stumpe, M. C., Wu, D., Narayanaswamy, A., Venugopalan, S., Widner, K., Madams, T., Cuadros, J., Kim, R., Raman, R., Nelson, P. C., Mega, J. L., & Webster, D. R. (2016). "Development and validation of a deep learning algorithm for detection of diabetic retinopathy in retinal fundus photographs." JAMA, 316(22), 2402–2410. https://doi.org/10.1001/jama.2016.17216

Gunning, D. (2017). "Explainable Artificial Intelligence (XAI) [Program brief]. Defense Advanced Research Projects Agency (DARPA)." https://www.darpa.mil/program/explainable-artificial-intelligence

Gunning, D., & Aha, D. (2019). DARPA's Explainable Artificial Intelligence (XAI) Program. *AI Magazine*, 40(2), 44–58. https://doi.org/10.1609/aimag.v40i2.2850

Mayo Clinic. (2019, September 10). "Mayo Clinic selects Google as strategic partner for health care innovation, cloud computing [Press release]." https://newsnetwork.mayoclinic.org/discussion/mayo-clinic-selects-google-as-strategic-partner-for-health-care-innovation-cloud-computing/

Ross, C., & Swetlitz, I. (2017, September 5). "IBM pitched its Watson supercomputer as a revolution in cancer care. It's nowhere close." STAT News. https://www.statnews.com/2017/09/05/watson-ibm-cancer/

Smith, B., & Shum, H. (2018). "The future computed: Artificial intelligence and its role in society." Microsoft. https://news.microsoft.com/futurecomputed/ — see also Microsoft's ongoing Responsible AI principles: https://www.microsoft.com/en-us/ai/principles-and-approach

Chapter 19

AI and Precision Medicine: Tailoring Treatments to the Individual

Precision medicine represents a paradigm shift in healthcare, moving away from a one-size-fits-all approach to treatments tailored to individual patients based on their genetic, environmental, and lifestyle factors. Artificial Intelligence (AI) is a driving force behind this transformation, enabling more accurate diagnoses, personalized treatment plans, and improved patient outcomes. This chapter explores the integration of AI and precision medicine, highlighting key technologies, real-world examples, challenges, and practical strategies for implementation.

The Promise of Precision Medicine

Precision medicine aims to provide the right treatment to the right patient at the right time. By leveraging AI, healthcare

DOI: 10.4324/9781003571407-24

providers can analyze vast amounts of data to uncover patterns and insights that inform personalized care.

Key Technologies in Precision Medicine:

1. **Genomic Sequencing:** Advances in genomic sequencing allow for detailed analysis of a patient's genetic makeup, identifying mutations and genetic predispositions to certain diseases.
2. **AI-Driven Data Analysis:** AI algorithms can analyze complex datasets, including genomic, clinical, and environmental data, to identify patterns and make predictions.
3. **Electronic Health Records (EHRs):** EHRs provide comprehensive patient data that AI can use to develop personalized treatment plans based on individual health histories.
4. **Wearable Devices:** Wearable devices collect real-time health data, such as heart rate and activity levels, which AI can analyze to monitor and adjust treatment plans dynamically.

Example: Tempus. Tempus is a technology company that uses AI to analyze clinical and molecular data to provide personalized cancer treatment recommendations. By integrating genomic sequencing data with clinical information, Tempus's AI platform identifies the most effective treatment options for individual patients.

Outcomes:

- **Improved Outcomes:** Patients receive treatments tailored to their genetic profiles, leading to better clinical outcomes.
- **Reduced Trial and Error:** AI reduces the trial-and-error approach in cancer treatment, saving time and reducing side effects.

- **Enhanced Research:** The data collected and analyzed by Tempus contributes to ongoing cancer research and the development of new therapies.

Key Takeaway: AI-driven precision medicine can significantly improve patient outcomes by tailoring treatments to individual needs and genetic profiles.

Real-World Applications of AI in Precision Medicine

Use Case: Personalized Cancer Treatment

Example: Foundation Medicine. Foundation Medicine uses AI to analyze genomic data from cancer patients and provide personalized treatment recommendations. The company's AI platform, FoundationOne, sequences the DNA of tumor samples to identify genetic mutations and match patients with targeted therapies and clinical trials.

Outcomes:

- **Targeted Therapies:** AI helps identify the most effective targeted therapies for individual patients based on their genetic profiles.
- **Clinical Trials:** Patients are matched with relevant clinical trials, providing access to cutting-edge treatments.
- **Improved Survival Rates:** Personalized treatment plans have led to improved survival rates and quality of life for cancer patients.

Key Takeaway: AI-powered genomic analysis can enhance cancer treatment by identifying targeted therapies and matching patients with clinical trials.

Use Case: Predictive Analytics for Disease Prevention

Example: 23andMe. 23andMe is a consumer genetics company that uses AI to analyze genetic data and provide personalized health insights. By examining a person's genetic predispositions, 23andMe's AI algorithms can predict the likelihood of developing certain diseases and recommend preventive measures.

Outcomes:

- **Early Detection:** AI predicts genetic risks, enabling early detection and intervention for diseases like cancer and cardiovascular conditions.
- **Preventive Care:** Personalized recommendations for lifestyle changes and preventive care help reduce the risk of developing diseases.
- **Patient Empowerment:** Individuals gain valuable insights into their genetic health, empowering them to make informed decisions about their health.

Key Takeaway: AI-driven predictive analytics can empower individuals with personalized health insights, promoting early detection and preventive care.

Challenges and Considerations

While AI and precision medicine offer significant benefits, several challenges must be addressed to ensure successful implementation.

Data Quality and Integration

High-quality, comprehensive data is essential for accurate AI predictions. Integrating diverse data sources, such as genomic, clinical, and lifestyle data, poses significant challenges.

Challenges:

- **Data Silos:** Data is often stored in separate silos, making integration difficult.
- **Data Quality:** Inconsistent or incomplete data can lead to inaccurate predictions and suboptimal outcomes.

Solutions:

- **Data Harmonization:** Implement data harmonization techniques to standardize and integrate data from multiple sources.
- **Quality Control:** Establish rigorous data quality control measures to ensure the accuracy and reliability of data.

Example: The Cancer Genome Atlas (TCGA). TCGA is a comprehensive cancer database that integrates genomic, clinical, and pathological data. By standardizing data collection and curation processes, TCGA provides high-quality data for AI-driven cancer research.

Outcomes:

- **Enhanced Research:** High-quality, integrated data supports advanced AI research and the development of personalized cancer treatments.
- **Collaborative Efforts:** TCGA's standardized data facilitates collaboration among researchers and healthcare providers.

Key Takeaway: Ensuring data quality and integration is critical for the success of AI-driven precision medicine.

Ethical and Privacy Concerns

The use of genetic and personal health data in AI raises significant ethical and privacy concerns. Ensuring patient consent, data security, and equitable access are paramount.

Challenges:

- **Privacy Risks:** Genetic data is highly sensitive and poses significant privacy risks if not adequately protected.
- **Ethical Considerations:** Issues such as informed consent, data ownership, and potential misuse of genetic information must be addressed.

Solutions:

- **Robust Security Measures:** Implement advanced encryption, access controls, and other security measures to protect patient data.
- **Ethical Guidelines:** Develop and adhere to ethical guidelines that prioritize patient consent, data ownership, and equitable access.

Example: GDPR Compliance in Genomic Research. The General Data Protection Regulation (GDPR) sets stringent standards for data protection and privacy in the European Union. Genomic research projects in Europe must comply with GDPR, ensuring robust data protection and ethical practices.

Outcomes:

- **Enhanced Trust:** Strong data protection measures build trust among patients and participants.
- **Ethical Research:** Compliance with ethical guidelines ensures responsible and equitable use of genetic data.

Key Takeaway: Addressing ethical and privacy concerns is essential for the responsible use of AI in precision medicine.

Practical Do's and Don'ts for Implementing AI in Precision Medicine

Do's:

1. **Do Ensure Data Quality:** Invest in high-quality data collection, harmonization, and quality control processes to ensure accurate AI predictions.
2. **Do Protect Privacy:** Implement robust data privacy and security measures to protect patient information and comply with regulations.
3. **Do Engage Patients:** Involve patients in the decision-making process, ensuring informed consent and transparency in the use of their genetic data.
4. **Do Foster Collaboration:** Encourage collaboration among researchers, healthcare providers, and technology developers to drive innovation and improve outcomes.
5. **Do Focus on Equity:** Ensure that the benefits of AI-driven precision medicine are accessible to all, including underserved and marginalized populations.

Don'ts:

1. **Don't Ignore Data Integration:** Neglecting data integration can lead to incomplete or inaccurate predictions. Invest in integrating diverse data sources.
2. **Don't Overlook Ethical Considerations:** Address ethical issues such as consent, data ownership, and potential misuse of genetic information.
3. **Don't Neglect Training:** Provide training for healthcare professionals on using AI tools and interpreting AI-driven insights.
4. **Don't Underestimate the Complexity:** Recognize the complexity of implementing AI in precision medicine and allocate sufficient resources and expertise.

5. **Don't Exclude Stakeholders:** Involve diverse stakeholders, including patients, ethicists, and community representatives, in the development and evaluation of AI solutions.

Conclusion

AI is revolutionizing precision medicine, enabling personalized treatments and improving patient outcomes. By leveraging key technologies, addressing challenges, and adhering to ethical principles, healthcare organizations can harness the power of AI to deliver more effective and personalized care. The future of precision medicine lies in the successful integration of AI, and with thoughtful planning and execution, its transformative potential can be fully realized.

Bibliography

23andMe, Inc. (n.d.). "Personalized genetic reports." https://www.23andme.com/dna-reports-list/

European Parliament and Council of the European Union. (2016). "Regulation (EU) 2016/679 of the European Parliament and of the Council of 27 April 2016 on the protection of natural persons with regard to the processing of personal data and on the free movement of such data, and repealing Directive 95/46/EC (General Data Protection Regulation)." Official Journal of the European Union, L 119/1. https://eur-lex.europa.eu/eli/reg/2016/679/oj (Enforced 25 May 2018.)

Foundation Medicine, Inc. (n.d.). "FoundationOne CDx — Comprehensive genomic profiling for solid tumors." https://www.foundationmedicine.com/test/foundationone-cdx

Gulshan, V., Peng, L., Coram, M., Stumpe, M. C., Wu, D., Narayanaswamy, A., Venugopalan, S., Widner, K., Madams, T., Cuadros, J., Kim, R., Raman, R., Nelson, P. C., Mega, J. L., & Webster, D. R. (2016). "Development and validation of a deep learning algorithm for detection of diabetic retinopathy in retinal fundus photographs." JAMA, 316(22), 2402–2410. https://doi.org/10.1001/jama.2016.17216

National Cancer Institute, Center for Cancer Genomics. (n.d.). "The Cancer Genome Atlas Program (TCGA)." https://www.cancer.gov/ccg/research/genome-sequencing/tcga — Genomic Data Commons portal: https://portal.gdc.cancer.gov/

Tempus AI, Inc. (n.d.). "Tempus — AI-powered precision medicine and genomic testing." https://www.tempus.com/

Chapter 20

Navigating the Regulatory Landscape of AI in Healthcare

As Artificial Intelligence (AI) continues to integrate into healthcare, navigating the regulatory landscape becomes increasingly crucial. Regulatory bodies worldwide are developing frameworks to ensure that AI technologies are safe, effective, and ethically deployed. This chapter explores the current state of AI regulation in healthcare, the challenges and opportunities it presents, and practical strategies for compliance and advocacy.

The Importance of Regulation in AI Healthcare

Regulation is essential for ensuring that AI technologies in healthcare are safe, reliable, and equitable. Well-designed regulatory frameworks can foster innovation while protecting patient rights and maintaining public trust.

DOI: 10.4324/9781003571407-25

Key Regulatory Objectives:

1. **Safety and Efficacy:** Ensuring that AI systems are safe and provide accurate, reliable results.
2. **Ethical Standards:** Promoting ethical practices, including fairness, transparency, and accountability.
3. **Data Privacy:** Protecting patient data privacy and ensuring compliance with data protection laws.
4. **Public Trust:** Building and maintaining public trust in AI technologies through rigorous oversight and transparency.

Current Regulatory Frameworks

Several regulatory bodies and frameworks guide the development and deployment of AI in healthcare. Understanding these frameworks is essential for navigating the regulatory landscape.

United States: FDA's Approach to AI in Healthcare

The U.S. Food and Drug Administration (FDA) plays a critical role in regulating medical devices, including AI-based technologies. The FDA has developed a framework to assess the safety and efficacy of AI systems.

Key Components:

- **Premarket Review:** AI systems classified as medical devices must undergo premarket review to ensure they meet safety and efficacy standards.
- **Good Machine Learning Practice (GMLP):** The FDA promotes GMLP, focusing on principles such as data quality, algorithm transparency, and continuous learning.
- **Real-World Evidence:** The FDA encourages the use of real-world evidence to monitor the performance of AI systems post-market.

Example: The FDA approved an AI algorithm developed by IDx-DR for the detection of diabetic retinopathy. The approval process involved rigorous evaluation of clinical trial data to ensure the algorithm's safety and effectiveness.

European Union: GDPR and AI Regulation

The General Data Protection Regulation (GDPR) sets stringent data protection standards in the European Union, impacting how AI systems handle patient data.

Key Components:

- **Data Minimization:** AI systems must collect only the data necessary for their purpose.
- **Consent:** Patients must provide informed consent for the use of their data.
- **Data Rights:** Patients have rights to access, rectify, and erase their data.

Example: AI systems used in the European Union must comply with GDPR, ensuring robust data privacy and protection. This includes obtaining explicit consent from patients for data processing.

International Standards: ISO and IEC

The International Organization for Standardization (ISO) and the International Electrotechnical Commission (IEC) develop global standards for AI and healthcare technologies.

Key Components:

- **ISO/IEC JTC 1/SC 42:** This committee focuses on AI standardization, including data quality, transparency, and risk management.

- **ISO 13485:** This standard specifies requirements for quality management systems for medical devices, including AI-based systems.

Example: Adopting ISO and IEC standards helps organizations ensure their AI systems meet international quality and safety benchmarks, facilitating global market access.

Challenges in AI Regulation

Regulating AI in healthcare presents unique challenges that require adaptive and forward-thinking approaches.

Rapid Technological Advancement

AI technologies evolve rapidly, often outpacing the development of regulatory frameworks. Regulators must balance the need for innovation with ensuring safety and efficacy.

Challenge:

- Keeping regulations up to date with technological advancements is challenging, potentially leading to regulatory gaps.

Solution:

- Developing adaptive regulatory frameworks that can evolve with technological changes and incorporating mechanisms for continuous learning and post-market surveillance.

Transparency and Explainability

AI systems, particularly deep learning models, often function as "black boxes," making it difficult to understand their decision-making processes.

Challenge:

- Lack of transparency and explainability can hinder regulatory approval and reduce trust among healthcare professionals and patients.

Solution:

- Promoting explainable AI (XAI) and requiring developers to provide clear, interpretable explanations of their AI systems' decision-making processes.

Data Privacy and Security

Ensuring data privacy and security is paramount, especially given the sensitive nature of healthcare data.

Challenge:

- Protecting patient data while enabling the use of AI for medical research and treatment.

Solution:

- Implementing robust data protection measures, complying with data privacy laws, and adopting privacy-preserving AI techniques such as federated learning and differential privacy.

Opportunities in AI Regulation

Effective regulation can create opportunities for innovation, market growth, and improved patient outcomes.

Fostering Innovation

Regulatory frameworks that support innovation can help bring safe and effective AI technologies to market more quickly.

Opportunity:

- Streamlining regulatory processes for AI-based medical devices can accelerate innovation and improve patient access to advanced technologies.

Example: The FDA's Digital Health Innovation Action Plan aims to foster innovation by providing clear regulatory pathways for digital health technologies, including AI.

Enhancing Global Collaboration

International collaboration on AI regulation can harmonize standards and facilitate the global adoption of AI technologies.

Opportunity:

- Harmonizing regulatory standards can reduce barriers to market entry and promote the global dissemination of AI innovations.

Example: The International Medical Device Regulators Forum (IMDRF) works toward harmonizing medical device regulations, including those for AI, across different countries.

Practical Strategies for Navigating AI Regulation

To successfully navigate the regulatory landscape, healthcare organizations and AI developers should adopt proactive and informed strategies.

Stay Informed and Engaged

Keeping abreast of regulatory developments and actively engaging with regulatory bodies is crucial for compliance and advocacy.

Strategy:

- Subscribe to regulatory updates, participate in industry forums, and engage with regulatory authorities to stay informed about changes in AI regulation.

Example: Joining industry associations and attending regulatory workshops can provide valuable insights and networking opportunities with regulators and peers.

Implement Good Machine Learning Practices (GMLP)

Adhering to GMLP ensures that AI systems are developed and deployed in compliance with regulatory standards.

Strategy:

- Follow best practices in data quality, algorithm development, validation, and monitoring to ensure AI systems meet safety and efficacy standards.

Example: Implementing rigorous validation and testing protocols during AI development to ensure robust performance and compliance with regulatory requirements.

Prioritize Data Privacy and Security

Ensuring data privacy and security is essential for regulatory compliance and maintaining patient trust.

Strategy:

- Implement robust data protection measures, including encryption, access controls, and regular security audits, to safeguard patient data.

Example: Adopting privacy-preserving AI techniques, such as federated learning, to train AI models without compromising patient data privacy.

Conclusion

Navigating the regulatory landscape of AI in healthcare is complex but essential for ensuring the safe, effective, and ethical use of AI technologies. By understanding current regulatory frameworks, addressing challenges, and adopting proactive strategies, healthcare organizations and AI developers can successfully bring innovative AI solutions to market. Effective regulation not only protects patients but also fosters innovation and enhances the overall impact of AI in healthcare.

The future of AI in healthcare is bright, and with thoughtful regulation, we can harness its full potential to transform patient care, improve health outcomes, and create a more equitable healthcare system.

Bibliography

Abràmoff, M. D., Lavin, P. T., Birch, M., Shah, N., & Folk, J. C. (2018). Pivotal trial of an autonomous AI-based diagnostic system for detection of diabetic retinopathy in primary care offices. *npj Digital Medicine*, 1, 39. https://doi.org/10.1038/s41746-018-0040-6

European Parliament and Council of the European Union. (2016). "Regulation (EU) 2016/679 (General Data Protection Regulation)." Official Journal of the European Union, L 119/1. https://eur-lex.europa.eu/eli/reg/2016/679/oj (Enforced 25 May 2018.)

International Medical Device Regulators Forum. (n.d.). "IMDRF — Harmonizing medical device regulations." https://www.imdrf.org/ — AI-specific: Machine Learning-enabled Medical Devices: Key Terms and Definitions (2022). https://www.imdrf.org/documents/machine-learning-enabled-medical-devices-key-terms-and-definitions

International Organization for Standardization. (n.d.). "ISO/IEC JTC 1/SC 42 — Artificial intelligence." https://www.iso.org/committee/6794475.html

U.S. Food and Drug Administration. (2017). "Digital health innovation action plan." https://www.fda.gov/media/106331/download

U.S. Food and Drug Administration. (2018, April 11). "FDA permits marketing of artificial intelligence-based device to detect certain diabetes-related eye problems [Press release]." https://www.fda.gov/news-events/press-announcements/fda-permits-marketing-artificial-intelligence-based-device-detect-certain-diabetes-related-eye (IDx-DR, the first FDA-approved autonomous AI diagnostic.)

Closing Chapter: The Future of AI in Healthcare: Embracing the Unseen Potential

As we draw this exploration of Artificial Intelligence (AI) in healthcare to a close, it is clear that AI holds transformative potential for the industry. From enhancing diagnostics and personalized medicine to improving operational efficiency and expanding access to care, AI is poised to revolutionize how we approach health and wellness. This closing chapter summarizes the key insights from our journey, highlights the challenges and opportunities ahead, and envisions the future of AI in healthcare.

Key Insights and Takeaways

1. **Transformative Potential of AI**

   AI has the power to transform every facet of healthcare. From precision medicine and AI-driven diagnostics to telehealth and global health initiatives, AI can enhance patient care, streamline operations, and address healthcare disparities. The integration of AI in healthcare

DOI: 10.4324/9781003571407-26

is not just a technological advancement but a paradigm shift toward a more efficient, equitable, and patient-centric healthcare system.

2. **Challenges and Ethical Considerations**

   The journey of AI in healthcare is fraught with challenges. Data quality, privacy, and integration are critical hurdles that must be overcome to ensure the effectiveness of AI solutions. Ethical considerations, such as bias, transparency, and accountability, are paramount to building trust and ensuring fair outcomes. Addressing these challenges requires a collaborative effort among healthcare providers, technologists, policymakers, and patients.

3. **Collaboration and Interdisciplinary Approach**

   Successful implementation of AI in healthcare hinges on collaboration across disciplines. Healthcare professionals, data scientists, ethicists, and technologists must work together to develop AI systems that are effective, ethical, and aligned with clinical needs. Interdisciplinary collaboration fosters innovation and ensures that AI solutions are practical and patient-focused.

4. **The Role of Data**

   Data is the backbone of AI. High-quality, diverse, and integrated datasets are essential for training accurate AI models. Investing in robust data infrastructure, ensuring data privacy, and promoting data sharing within ethical and legal frameworks are critical steps toward harnessing the full potential of AI.

5. **Patient-Centric AI**

   At the heart of AI in healthcare is the patient. AI solutions must be designed with the patient in mind, enhancing patient outcomes, empowering individuals with personalized insights, and ensuring equitable access to AI-driven healthcare services. Patient engagement and education are vital for the successful adoption of AI technologies.

The Road Ahead: Opportunities and Vision

As we look into the future, the opportunities for AI in healthcare are boundless. The ongoing advancements in AI technologies, combined with an increasing understanding of human health and disease, will continue to push the boundaries of what is possible.

1. **Continuous Innovation**
   The pace of innovation in AI and healthcare will only accelerate. Emerging technologies such as explainable AI, quantum computing, and advanced robotics will open new frontiers in medical research, diagnostics, and treatment. Continuous innovation will drive improvements in patient care and operational efficiency.
2. **Global Impact**
   AI has the potential to address global health challenges, bridging the healthcare divide and bringing quality care to underserved populations. By leveraging AI for disease surveillance, telehealth, and remote monitoring, healthcare can become more accessible and equitable worldwide.
3. **Ethical AI Development**
   The future of AI in healthcare must be rooted in ethical principles. Ensuring fairness, transparency, and accountability in AI development will be crucial for building trust and maximizing the positive impact of AI. Ongoing dialogue and collaboration among stakeholders will be essential for navigating the ethical landscape of AI.
4. **Personalized and Preventive Care**
   AI will continue to advance personalized and preventive care, shifting the focus from reactive to proactive healthcare. By analyzing genetic, environmental, and lifestyle data, AI can predict and prevent diseases, tailor treatments to individual needs, and promote overall health and wellness.

5. **Empowered Healthcare Workforce**
   AI will augment the capabilities of healthcare professionals, enabling them to focus on high-value tasks and improving their productivity and job satisfaction. Investing in AI education and training for the healthcare workforce will be critical for harnessing the benefits of AI.

Embracing the Future

The integration of AI in healthcare is a journey filled with promise and potential. As we embrace this future, it is essential to remain committed to the principles of innovation, collaboration, and ethical responsibility. By doing so, we can unlock the unseen potential of AI and create a healthcare system that is more efficient, equitable, and patient-centered.

The path forward is clear: embrace AI with a spirit of curiosity and responsibility, focus on continuous improvement and innovation, and always keep the well-being of patients at the forefront. The future of AI in healthcare is bright, and together, we can transform healthcare for the better, making a lasting impact on the lives of individuals and communities around the world.

Final Thoughts

As we conclude this book, it is evident that the journey of AI in healthcare is just beginning. The insights, examples, and strategies discussed in these chapters are stepping stones toward a future where AI plays a central role in delivering high-quality, personalized, and accessible healthcare. The potential of AI is vast, and by embracing its possibilities with a commitment to ethical principles and collaborative innovation, we can create a healthcare system that meets the needs of all patients and fosters a healthier world.

Thank you for joining us on this journey. The future of AI in healthcare is a collective endeavor, and together, we can make it a reality.

Bibliography

23andMe, Inc. (2024). “Health + Ancestry Service: Reports list.” 23andMe. https://www.23andme.com/dna-reports-list/

European Parliament and Council of the European Union. (2016). “Regulation (EU) 2016/679 of the European Parliament and of the Council of 27 April 2016 on the protection of natural persons with regard to the processing of personal data and on the free movement of such data, and repealing Directive 95/46/EC (General Data Protection Regulation).” Official Journal of the European Union, L 119, 1–88. https://eur-lex.europa.eu/eli/reg/2016/679/oj

Foundation Medicine. (2024). “FoundationOne®CDx: Comprehensive genomic profiling”. Foundation Medicine, Inc. https://www.foundationmedicine.com/test/foundationone-cdx

Gulshan, V., Peng, L., Coram, M., Stumpe, M. C., Wu, D., Narayanaswamy, A., Venugopalan, S., Widner, K., Madams, T., Cuadros, J., Kim, R., Raman, R., Nelson, P. C., Mega, J. L., & Webb, R. (2016). “Development and validation of a deep learning algorithm for detection of diabetic retinopathy in retinal fundus photographs.” JAMA, 316(22), 2402–2410. https://doi.org/10.1001/jama.2016.17216

Mayo Clinic. (2019, September 10). “Mayo Clinic selects Google as strategic partner for health care innovation, cloud computing [Press release].” Mayo Clinic News Network. https://newsroom.mayoclinic.org/2019/09/10/mayo-clinic-selects-google-as-strategic-partner-for-health-care-innovation-cloud-computing/

National Cancer Institute. (n.d.). "The Cancer Genome Atlas Program (TCGA)." Center for Cancer Genomics, NCI. https://www.cancer.gov/ccg/research/genome-sequencing/tcga

Smith, B., & Shum, H. (2018). "The Future Computed: Artificial Intelligence and its Role in Society." Microsoft Corporation. https://news.microsoft.com/futurecomputed/

Tempus AI, Inc. (2024). *Intelligent diagnostics: Tempus platform.* Tempus. https://www.tempus.com/

Appendices

Note: How to Navigate the Appendices

The appendices are designed to be used flexibly. Readers may move through them linearly or reference them selectively based on their role, interests, or stage of engagement with AI in healthcare.

Use the guidance below to find the most relevant sections quickly:

- ***If you are new to AI or healthcare terminology***
  *Start with **Appendix A: Glossary of AI and Healthcare Terms**. This appendix establishes a shared vocabulary used throughout the book and is especially helpful when reading Parts I, III, and IV.*
- ***If you want to understand how AI works beneath the surface***
  *See **Appendix B: Technical Overview of AI in Healthcare**. This section explains core AI methods, architectures, and evaluation concepts that underpin the real-world use cases discussed across the book.*
- ***If you are concerned about ethics, bias, regulation, or trust***
  *Go to **Appendix C: Ethical Frameworks and Guidelines**. This appendix provides practical framing for responsible AI development and governance, complementing the discussions in Part III.*

- ***If you are building, evaluating, or researching AI solutions***
  Review ***Appendix D: Data Sources and Datasets*** *and* ***Appendix E: Practical Tools and Resources****. These appendices support applied work, implementation planning, and execution.*
- ***If you want to explore beyond the book***
  Start with ***Appendix F: Further Reading and References****, which curates books, articles, and evolving online resources aligned to the book's major themes.*

Together, the appendices are intended to function as a reference system that supports both understanding and action, alongside the main chapters.

* * *

The appendices of *AI in Healthcare: Bridging the Present and Future* are designed to serve as a practical and intellectual extension of the main text. While the chapters focus on narrative, strategy, and real-world impact, the appendices provide structured reference material, deeper technical context, and actionable resources for readers who wish to go further.

Taken together, these sections support three core goals:

1. **Accessibility** – ensuring readers from diverse backgrounds can engage with AI and healthcare concepts confidently
2. **Depth** – offering additional technical, ethical, and methodological detail without disrupting the flow of the main narrative
3. **Practical Enablement** – equipping leaders, clinicians, technologists, and policymakers with tools they can apply in real settings

Readers may approach the appendices linearly or use them selectively as reference material throughout their journey with the book.

Appendix A: Glossary of AI and Healthcare Terms

This glossary defines key terms and concepts used throughout the book, providing a common language for readers across clinical, technical, business, and policy domains. Given the interdisciplinary nature of AI in healthcare, terminology often carries different meanings depending on context; this glossary is intended to reduce ambiguity and promote shared understanding.

Related Chapters: Chapters 1–2, 9–11, 13–20

Readers may find this appendix especially helpful when engaging with:

- **Part I (Chapters 1–2)**, which introduces foundational AI concepts and historical context
- **Part III (Chapters 9–11)**, where ethical, regulatory, and implementation language becomes more precise
- **Part IV (Chapters 13–20)**, where advanced and future-oriented terminology is introduced

The glossary is intended to be referenced throughout the book rather than read sequentially.

Artificial Intelligence (AI) A broad field of computer science focused on creating systems capable of performing tasks that typically require human intelligence, such as reasoning, perception, learning, and decision-making.

Machine Learning (ML) A subset of AI in which algorithms learn patterns from data and improve performance over time without being explicitly programmed.

Deep Learning A class of machine learning techniques based on multi-layered neural networks *(computational models inspired by interconnected neurons in the human* *brain)* particularly effective in image recognition, natural language processing, and complex pattern detection.

Electronic Health Records (EHRs) Digital versions of patients' medical histories, including diagnoses, medications, lab results, and clinical notes, maintained across healthcare organizations.

Genomic Sequencing The process of determining the complete DNA sequence of an organism, enabling insights into disease risk, treatment response, and personalized medicine.

Natural Language Processing (NLP) AI techniques that enable computers to understand, interpret, and generate human language, widely used in clinical documentation, medical coding, and literature review.

Predictive Analytics The use of historical and real-time data, statistical methods, and AI models to forecast future outcomes, such as disease risk or hospital readmissions.

Telehealth The delivery of healthcare services remotely through digital communication technologies, including video visits, remote monitoring, and virtual care platforms.

Precision Medicine An approach to healthcare that tailors prevention, diagnosis, and treatment to individual variability in genes, environment, and lifestyle.

Explainable AI (XAI) Methods and systems that make AI decisions interpretable and understandable to humans, particularly important in regulated and high-stakes environments like healthcare.

Bias in AI Systematic errors in AI outputs that result from biased data, flawed assumptions, or inequitable design, potentially leading to unequal outcomes across populations.

Ethical AI The development and deployment of AI systems in ways that prioritize fairness, transparency, accountability, privacy, and human well-being.

Data Privacy and Security The practices, technologies, and regulations that protect sensitive health information from unauthorized access, misuse, or breaches.

Appendix B: Technical Overview of AI in Healthcare

Related Chapters: Chapters 3–8, 11, 13–19

This appendix provides a deeper technical foundation for readers who want to understand *how* AI systems function beneath the surface. While the main chapters emphasize applications and outcomes, this section explains the underlying algorithms, architectures, and evaluation techniques that make those outcomes possible.

This appendix directly supports:

- **Part II (Chapters 3–8)**, which explores AI use cases across providers, payers, pharmacies, life sciences, and medical devices
- **Chapter 11**, which discusses implementation challenges related to data quality, model performance, and system integration
- **Part IV (Chapters 13–19)**, where advanced AI capabilities such as predictive analytics, personalization, and autonomous systems are discussed

Technical readers may wish to review this appendix alongside relevant case studies in the main text.

Machine Learning Algorithms

Supervised Learning Models trained on labeled datasets to predict known outcomes, commonly used in diagnostics, risk stratification, and claims prediction.

Unsupervised Learning Techniques that identify hidden patterns or groupings in unlabeled data, useful for patient segmentation, anomaly detection, and population health insights.

Reinforcement Learning Algorithms that learn optimal actions through trial and feedback, increasingly applied in treatment optimization, resource allocation, and adaptive clinical workflows.

Deep Learning Architectures

Convolutional Neural Networks (CNNs) Optimized for image and spatial data, widely used in radiology, pathology, and medical imaging diagnostics.

Recurrent Neural Networks (RNNs) Designed for sequential data, such as time-series vitals or longitudinal patient records.

Generative Adversarial Networks (GANs) Models that generate synthetic data, with applications in data augmentation, privacy-preserving research, and medical image generation.

Data Preprocessing Techniques

Data Cleaning – Addressing missing, inconsistent, or erroneous data

Data Normalization – Ensuring comparability across sources and scales

Feature Engineering – Transforming raw data into meaningful model inputs

Model Evaluation Metrics

Accuracy – Overall correctness of predictions

Precision and Recall – Tradeoffs between false positives and false negatives

F1 Score – Balanced measure of precision and recall

ROC-AUC – Ability to distinguish between outcome classes across thresholds

Appendix C: Ethical Frameworks and Guidelines

Related Chapters: Chapters 9, 10, 12, 15, 20

This appendix expands on the ethical principles and governance considerations introduced throughout the book. It provides structured frameworks, illustrative case studies, and curated resources to help organizations operationalize responsible AI.

It is most closely aligned with:

- **Chapter 9**, which examines bias, fairness, and trust in AI-driven healthcare
- **Chapter 10**, which addresses regulatory and compliance considerations
- **Chapter 12**, which explores economic tradeoffs and unintended consequences
- **Chapter 15**, which discusses global health implications and equity
- **Chapter 20**, which outlines strategic recommendations for future-ready leadership

Readers involved in governance, policy, compliance, or executive decision-making may find this appendix particularly valuable.

Principles of Ethical AI

- **Fairness** – Avoiding discriminatory outcomes
- **Transparency** – Making systems understandable to users and stakeholders
- **Accountability** – Defining responsibility for AI-driven decisions
- **Privacy** – Protecting patient autonomy and data rights

Case Studies of Ethical AI Implementation

- **Success Stories** highlighting equitable and transparent deployments

- **Lessons Learned** from failures, unintended consequences, and course corrections

Resources for Ethical AI

- Academic and industry publications (many of which are cited throughout the book)
- Global organizations and standards bodies
  - **World Health Organization (WHO)**

    The World Health Organization provides globally recognized guidance on the ethical use of artificial intelligence in health. Its work emphasizes patient safety, equity, transparency, and human oversight, offering a public-health perspective that is especially relevant for national health systems, policymakers, and global health initiatives.
  - **Organisation for Economic Co-operation and Development (OECD)**

    The OECD has developed widely adopted principles for trustworthy AI, focusing on human-centered values, robustness, accountability, and transparency. These principles are frequently referenced by governments and regulators and provide a practical bridge between ethical intent and policy implementation.
  - **International Organization for Standardization (ISO)**

    ISO develops international standards related to data governance, information security, and AI systems. Its work supports consistent, auditable approaches to risk management, quality assurance, and system reliability, making it particularly relevant for organizations seeking to operationalize ethical AI at scale.
- Practical toolkits for ethical assessment and governance
  - **AI Ethics Impact Assessment Frameworks**
    - Structured assessment tools designed to evaluate potential risks related to bias, fairness,

explainability, and unintended consequences before and during AI deployment. These frameworks help organizations move from abstract principles to concrete decision-making checkpoints across the AI lifecycle. For example:

- **Algorithmic Impact Assessment (AIA)** developed by the **Government of Canada**, which requires organizations to assess potential impacts of automated decision systems across areas such as human rights, transparency, data governance, and accountability before deployment. The framework provides a structured, repeatable approach to risk classification, mitigation planning, and ongoing oversight, and has influenced similar efforts in both public- and private-sector AI governance.
- **UK Information Commissioner's Office (ICO) –** AI and Data Protection Impact Assessment Guidance
- **European Commission –** Ethics Guidelines for Trustworthy AI (Operational Assessment Lists)

– **Model Cards and Documentation Practices**

Standardized approaches for documenting AI models, including intended use, limitations, training data characteristics, and known risks. These practices promote transparency and shared understanding among developers, clinicians, executives, and regulators.

– **Algorithmic Auditing and Monitoring Playbooks**

Operational guides that outline how to test, monitor, and periodically reassess AI systems for performance drift, bias, and compliance over time. These toolkits emphasize continuous governance rather than one-time approval, aligning closely with the real-world challenges discussed in the book.

Appendix D: Data Sources and Datasets

Related Chapters: Chapters 3–8, 11, 13–19

This appendix catalogs key public and clinical datasets commonly used in healthcare AI research and development. It is intended as a practical reference for practitioners, researchers, and innovators seeking real-world data sources.

This appendix supports:

- **Part II (Chapters 3–8)**, where real-world AI applications depend on diverse clinical and operational data
- **Chapter 11**, which discusses challenges related to data fragmentation and quality
- **Part IV (Chapters 13–19)**, where future AI capabilities depend on increasingly rich, longitudinal, and multimodal datasets

Readers should note that access requirements, governance constraints, and ethical considerations vary significantly across datasets.

Public Health Databases

- Centers for Disease Control and Prevention (CDC)
- World Health Organization (WHO)
- National Institutes of Health (NIH)

Genomic Databases

- The Cancer Genome Atlas (TCGA)
- Genotype-Tissue Expression (GTEx) Project
- 1000 Genomes Project

Clinical Datasets

- MIMIC-III Clinical Database
- UK Biobank
- OpenEHR repositories

Appendix E: Practical Tools and Resources

Related Chapters: Chapters 11, 12, 20

This appendix is designed to help readers translate ideas into action. It includes implementation guides, evaluation checklists, and software references that align with the execution challenges discussed in the book.

It directly complements:

- **Chapter 11**, which focuses on integration, change management, and adoption challenges
- **Chapter 12**, which examines ROI, cost-benefit analysis, and economic impact
- **Chapter 20**, which provides a forward-looking roadmap for executives and practitioners building AI capabilities

This appendix is especially relevant for healthcare leaders, transformation teams, and program owners responsible for delivering measurable results.

Implementation Guides

- Step-by-step approaches to deploying AI in healthcare settings
  - **NHS UK – A Guide to Implementing Artificial Intelligence in Health and Care**

    A practical implementation guide developed for healthcare organizations adopting AI solutions. It outlines a step-by-step journey from problem definition and data readiness through validation, deployment, monitoring, and scaling, with an emphasis on clinical safety, governance, and stakeholder engagement.
  - **World Health Organization (WHO) – Ethics and Governance of Artificial Intelligence for Health (Implementation Guidance)**

While grounded in ethics, this WHO guidance includes a clear, phased approach to introducing AI into health systems, covering readiness assessment, risk management, regulatory alignment, and ongoing evaluation. It is particularly relevant for health systems and policymakers implementing AI at scale.

- **U.S. Food and Drug Administration (FDA) – Good Machine Learning Practice (GMLP) for Medical Device Development**

  A set of publicly available principles jointly developed with international partners that describe best practices across the AI lifecycle, from data collection and model development to deployment and post-market monitoring. Although focused on regulated medical devices, the guidance is widely applicable to healthcare AI implementation more broadly.

■ Checklists for evaluating vendors, models, and use cases

- **NHS AI Lab – Buyer's Guide for AI in Health and Care**

  A practical checklist designed to help healthcare organizations evaluate AI vendors and solutions. It covers clinical relevance, evidence of effectiveness, data requirements, interoperability, regulatory compliance, and long-term support considerations.

- **Model Cards for Model Reporting (by Google Research, public framework)**

  A standardized checklist-style framework for documenting AI models, including intended use, performance characteristics, limitations, training data considerations, and ethical risks. While originally developed for general AI, it is frequently referenced in healthcare contexts as a transparency and evaluation tool.

- **Algorithmic Accountability and Transparency Checklists (New York City Automated Decision Systems Task Force)**

  A publicly released set of evaluation questions and transparency considerations designed to assess automated decision systems. The checklist focuses on governance, explainability, bias risk, and accountability, making it useful when evaluating AI use cases and vendor claims in healthcare settings.

Software and Tools

- **AI Platforms:** TensorFlow, PyTorch
- **Data Analysis:** Python, R
- **Visualization:** Tableau, Power BI

Best Practices

- Maintaining data quality and integrity
- Managing AI programs as long-term capabilities, not one-off projects
- Engaging clinicians, executives, and patients as active stakeholders

Appendix F: Further Reading and References

Related Chapters: All

This appendix provides a curated bibliography of books, academic articles, and online resources referenced throughout the book. It is intended for readers who wish to explore specific topics – technical, clinical, ethical, or strategic – in greater depth.

The materials listed here align broadly with:

- Historical foundations discussed in **Part I**
- Sector-specific applications in **Part II**

- Governance and economics in **Part III**
- Future-oriented innovation in **Part IV**

Books and Publications

- *Deep Medicine* – Eric Topol
- *AI in Health* – Tom Lawry
- *Machine Learning for Healthcare* – Kevin D. Johnson

Academic Articles

Peer-reviewed journals, conferences, and foundational research cited throughout the book.

Websites and Online Resources

The following websites and online resources provide ongoing insight into artificial intelligence, healthcare innovation, and the responsible use of advanced technologies. Unlike static books or papers, these platforms evolve continuously, reflecting new research, real-world deployments, regulatory shifts, and ethical debates.

They are grouped into three categories – **AI & Healthcare Innovation**, **Policy and Responsible AI**, and **Clinical Practice & Care Delivery** – followed by a short list of **Recommended First 5 Resources** for non-technical executives and leaders seeking a practical starting point.

AI and Healthcare Innovation

Stanford Medicine – Center for Artificial Intelligence in Medicine & Imaging (AIMI)

A leading academic center focused on translating AI research into clinical impact, particularly in imaging, diagnostics, and clinical decision support. AIMI publishes accessible summaries of current research, hosts educational events, and highlights real-world applications of AI across healthcare settings.

MIT Technology Review – AI and Health Coverage

An independent technology publication offering clear, balanced analysis of how AI is shaping healthcare, life sciences, and medicine. Coverage includes case studies, regulatory developments, ethical debates, and emerging trends, written for a broad, non-specialist audience.

Policy, Governance, and Responsible AI

World Health Organization (WHO) – *Artificial Intelligence for Health*

The WHO's *AI for Health* resources provide global guidance on governance, ethics, and responsible adoption of AI in healthcare. The site emphasizes patient safety, equity, transparency, and international collaboration, making it particularly valuable for policymakers and healthcare leaders operating at national or system-wide levels.

National Academy of Medicine (NAM) – Artificial Intelligence in Health Care

The National Academy of Medicine convenes experts across medicine, technology, and policy to examine how AI should be designed, evaluated, and governed in healthcare. Its work focuses on trust, accountability, and long-term societal impact rather than short-term technological novelty.

Partnership on AI

A multi-stakeholder organization that brings together industry, academia, nonprofits, and policymakers to advance responsible AI. Its healthcare-related work addresses fairness, bias, transparency, and real-world implementation challenges, offering practical frameworks rather than abstract principles.

Clinical Practice and Care Delivery

American Medical Association (AMA) – Augmented Intelligence in Health Care

The AMA's resources focus on how AI and automation affect physicians, clinical workflows, and patient care. The site emphasizes "augmented intelligence" – AI as a support tool rather than a replacement for clinicians – and provides guidance on adoption, trust, and professional responsibility.

BMJ Health & Care Informatics

An open-access journal and resource hub focused on digital health, clinical informatics, and data-driven care delivery. Content bridges clinical practice and technology, making it useful for clinicians, informaticists, and healthcare leaders evaluating AI in real-world care environments.

Recommended First 5 Resources (For Non-Technical Executives)

For readers who want a concise, high-quality entry point – without diving into technical detail – the following five resources provide the best balance of strategic insight, credibility, and accessibility:

1. **MIT Technology Review – AI & Health**
   A clear, executive-friendly view of where AI in healthcare is succeeding, struggling, and evolving.
2. **World Health Organization – AI for Health**
   The best starting point for understanding global norms, ethics, and policy considerations around AI in healthcare.
3. **Stanford AIMI**
   A practical window into how leading academic medical centers are actually applying AI in clinical settings.

4. **American Medical Association – Augmented Intelligence**
   Essential reading for understanding how AI affects clinicians, workflows, and trust at the point of care.
5. **National Academy of Medicine – AI in Health Care**
   A thoughtful, future-oriented perspective on governance, accountability, and long-term impact.
6. **How to Use These Resources**
   The resources listed in this appendix are intended to support different readers in different ways, depending on their role in the healthcare ecosystem. While all readers may benefit from exploring them broadly, the guidance below highlights how these resources align with specific themes and chapters in the book.
7. **For Executives and Senior Leaders**
   Executives should approach these resources as tools for sense-making rather than technical instruction. The goal is not to master algorithms, but to understand where AI is creating real value, where risks and constraints exist, and how governance, trust, and economics shape outcomes.
   High-level perspectives from sources such as *MIT Technology Review*, the *World Health Organization's AI for Health* materials, and the *National Academy of Medicine* are especially relevant when reading **Chapters 9** and **10**, which address ethics, regulation, and compliance, as well as **Chapter 12**, which explores economic impact and return on investment. These resources also reinforce the strategic recommendations discussed in **Chapter 20**, helping leaders connect near-term decisions to long-term organizational readiness.
8. **For Clinicians and Clinical Leaders**
   Clinicians should view these resources as aids to informed adoption rather than replacements for clinical judgment. Platforms such as the *American Medical Association's augmented intelligence resources* and *BMJ*

Health & Care Informatics are most relevant when reading **Chapter 3**, which focuses on AI in provider settings, and **Chapter 11**, which addresses implementation, workflow integration, and change management. These resources also complement future-oriented discussions in **Chapters 13** and **14**, where AI begins to play a more proactive role in diagnostics, treatment planning, and telehealth.

9. **For Policymakers and Governance Leaders**

   Readers focused on policy, regulation, and system-level oversight will find the *World Health Organization*, *Partnership on AI*, and *National Academy of Medicine* resources particularly useful alongside **Chapters 9** and **10**, which explore ethical frameworks and regulatory considerations, and **Chapter 15**, which examines global health implications. These resources provide broader context for balancing innovation with safety, equity, and public trust.

10. **For Cross-Functional Teams**

    For teams spanning clinical, technical, operational, and policy roles, these resources serve as a shared foundation that supports alignment across disciplines. They are especially valuable when engaging with **Chapter 11** on implementation challenges and **Chapter 20** on building future-ready AI strategies, where success depends less on any single function and more on coordinated execution.

    Used together with the main chapters, these resources help bridge theory and practice – supporting you the reader in not only in understanding AI in healthcare, but in applying it responsibly and effectively.

Index

For Product Safety Concerns and Information please contact our EU representative GPSR@taylorandfrancis.com
Taylor & Francis Verlag GmbH, Kaufingerstraße 24, 80331 München, Germany

www.ingramcontent.com/pod-product-compliance
Ingram Content Group UK Ltd.
Pitfield, Milton Keynes, MK11 3LW, UK
UKHW022116190926
475702UK00013B/1475

* 9 7 8 1 0 3 2 9 4 2 1 4 8 *